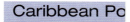Caribbean Pocket Natural History

Trees of Cuba

Angela T. Leiva Sánchez
Translated by Juliet Barclay
Photography by Gonzalo Canetti

MACMILLAN
CARIBBEAN

Macmillan Education
Between Towns Road, Oxford OX4 3PP
A division of Macmillan Publishers Limited
Companies and representatives throughout the world

www.macmillan-caribbean.com

ISBN: 978-1-4050-2905-6

Text ©Angela T. Leiva Sánchez 2007
Design and illustration © Macmillan Publishers Limited 2007

First published 2007

All rights reserved; no part of this publication may be reproduced, stored in a retrieval system, transmitted in any form or by any means, electronic, mechanical, photocopying, recording or otherwise, without the prior written permission of the publishers.

Designed by Carol Hulme
Typeset by Amanda Easter Design Ltd
Map by Tek-Art
Cover design Gary Fielder
Cover photography by Gonzalo Canetti
Commissioned photography by Gonzalo Canetti

Printed and bound in Malaysia

2011 2010 2009 2008 2007
10 9 8 7 6 5 4 3 2 1

Contents

Map of Cuba	iv
Introduction	v
The Trees Descriptive text and photographs	1
Glossary	101
Bibliography	102
Index of Common Names	103
Index of Scientific Names	105

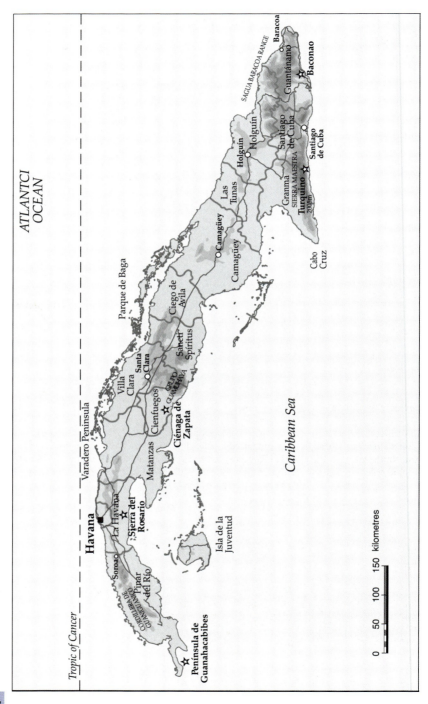

Introduction

This book has been produced not for academics but for anyone wishing to identify the most commonly seen trees in Cuba, whether they are in the city, beside the road, on the beach or in other parts of the island. There are well over 800 species of tree (native, naturalized and cultivated) growing on the island, and thus this slim volume presents only a sample of the enormous arboreal variety to be found in Cuba. Around twenty of these trees have such beautiful flowers that they are frequently planted for ornamental purposes and thus also appear in the companion volume, *Flowers of Cuba*. The reader will find both native and cultivated species, which have been balanced to present an objective guide.

In the Cuban landscape, both in the countryside and the city, palms play a major part and are very distinguished elements. This book contains those palms that the reader will almost certainly encounter in trips around Cuba.

The flowering times of the trees are listed as a result of direct observation by the author; however, it should be borne in mind that these dates tend to vary in the Tropics, even to the extent of finding two trees of the same species flowering at completely different times.

The descriptions are brief and concise and we have tried to avoid scientific terminology wherever possible. The book has a glossary to explain technical terms that we have been unable to avoid. The species appear in the alphabetical order of the common names by which they are known in Cuba. Wherever possible, we have also included other English (Caribbean) names of the species, and both these and the scientific names are listed in the indexes. The simple explanations and clear photographs will aid identification of species.

Cuba is part of an archipelago, and is the largest of the Greater Antilles in the West Indies. It is located to the south of the Tropic of Cancer between 74°8' and 84°58'W longitude and between 19°50' and 23°17'N latitude; 180 km (110 miles) south of Florida (USA) and 210 km (130 miles) east of Yucatán (Mexico); to the south, Jamaica is 140 km (87 miles) away and to the east only 77 km (48 miles) of ocean lie between Cuba and Haiti. The main island, Cuba, is long and narrow, extending in direction from the northwest to the southeast. It is 1 250 km (775 miles) long at its greatest extent and has 5 746 km (3 400 miles) of coastline with hundreds of beautiful beaches. Two-thirds of the island's land consists of plains. Cuba has four principal mountain ranges: the Guaniguanico in the west, which includes the smaller ranges of Los Órganos and del Rosario; the Guamuhaya in the centre of the island, with the smaller Escambray range; the large Sierra Maestra range in the southeast of the island, which contains the highest mountain in the country, Pico Turquino (1 974 m or 6 476 ft above sea level); and the Sagua–Baracoa range in the northeast, which contains the smaller ranges of Nipe, Cristal, Moa, Toa, Imías and Baracoa.

The Cuban climate is tropical with two seasons: the rainy season from May to October, and the dry season from November to April. The average annual temperature is 25°C (77°F), with a summer maximum of around 35°C (95°F) in July and an average minimum of 10°C (50°F) in December. Humidity tends to range between 74 and 80% during the day, and is often over 90% at night. Annual rainfall depends somewhat on hurricanes and cold fronts; the average figures lie between 1 100 and 1 600 mm (43 and 63 in) per year.

The Caribbean region is one of the most important areas among conservation priorities for the planet. It is considered to be one of the 25 hotspots (areas exhibiting exceptional concentrations of endemic species but facing exceptional loss of habitat) in the world. Cuba, which is the largest territory in the Caribbean, has the region's highest number of endemic plants and has suffered a tremendous destruction of natural habitats during its history, and thus contributes greatly to the consideration of the Caribbean region as an important hotspot.

Cuba has around 7 000 native plants, 51% of which are endemic to the country, which makes it one of the most richly endowed islands in the world. It also has a wide diversity of ecosystems, with eight major types of vegetation. The variety of soil types in the country and the height above sea level greatly contribute to the richness of its flora.

A total of 22% of the territory is under the protected areas system. Six Biosphere Reserves, two World Heritage areas and six Ramsar sites (wetlands) are among the most relevant protected areas.

Abrojo

(Abrojo de la Florida, Bella Hortensia)
Pereskia zinniiflora DC.

Synonym: *Rhodocactus cubensris* (Britton & Rose) F.M. Knuth

WARNING: Abrojo is a very prickly tree.

Family: Cactaceae

Origin: Cuba, endemic.

Height: A small, deciduous tree growing up to 4 m (13 ft) high.

Trunk: Straight, up to 25 cm (10 in) in diameter, with numerous short branches, very prickly.

Canopy: A rounded to narrow canopy. Abrojo is deciduous.

Leaves: Alternate, fleshy, elliptical to obovate, with sharp tips, 1.5–4 cm (½–1½ in) long. Dark green, shiny and smooth on both sides.

Flowers: Appearing singly with male and female flowers growing on different trees, deep pink to purple in colour. When the trees are in blossom, bees gravitate towards the flowers, making such a loud noise that from about 3 m (10 ft) away the tree itself appears to be buzzing. Blossoms in April to June.

Fruit: A berry of 2–3 cm (about 1 in) diameter that contains numerous small, black, angular seeds embedded in white flesh.

Comments: This is a beautiful – but sometimes harmful – tree that is very scarce and needs protection. In Cuba it is found in dry woodlands near the sea in the Eastern provinces, as well as in swampier woodland environments in the centre of the island, where it grows alongside *Copernicia* palms.

Adonidia

(Manila Palm)
Veitchia merrillii (Becc.) H.E. Moore

Synonym: *Adonidia merrillii* Becc.

Family: Arecaceae (Palmae)

Origin: Philippines.

Height: Up to 5 m (16 ft), usually much less.

Trunk: A single trunk, greyish, cylindrical but slightly tapering upward towards the crownshaft, closely and faintly ringed; 15–25 cm (6–10 in) diameter.

Canopy: Pinnate palm.

Leaves: Feathery, arched, bright green, about 50 pairs of segments in each leaf; crownshaft about 50 cm (20 in) long, smooth, pale green.

Flowers: In multi-branched bunches attached to stalks that emerge from below the crownshaft; the buds are pale green, the flowers yellowish-white. The tree bears numerous bunches of flowers in various stages of development, simultaneously throughout the year.

Fruit: Very attractive bright red, smooth fruits, almost round but with a small point, measuring 2–3 cm (¾–1 in) long. Each fruit contains one pale yellow oblong seed about 2 cm (¾ in) in diameter.

Comments: An ornamental palm used throughout Cuba, the Caribbean and in other tropical countries. Its small size and swift growth make it very useful for gardens and for urban planting.

Aguacate

(Avocado, Alligator Pear)
Persea americana Mill.

Synonym: *Persea gratisima* Gaernt.

Family: Lauraceae

Origin: Central and tropical South America.

Height: Up to 15 m (50 ft) in very old trees.

Trunk: Straight, with dark brown, furrowed bark.

Canopy: Rounded, transparent and deciduous.

Leaves: Growing alternately from the twigs, elliptical with pointed tips, dark green and shiny, about 15 cm (6 in) long and 7 cm (nearly 3 in) wide.

Flowers: Inconspicuous, greenish-white in colour, grouped in clusters. Slightly scented. Blossoms once a year, most commonly in April to May.

Fruit: The pear-shaped, elliptical or rounded fruit varies in size. The pulp is buttery, yellow at the centre and green around the outside, with a leathery skin that is green even when ripe. In some varieties the skin is deep purple. The fruit of the Aguacate contains a single, large, rounded seed at the centre.

Comments: The Spanish word 'aguacate' ('ahuacatl') comes from the Nahuatl language of the pre-Hispanic inhabitants of the area now known as Mexico. The English 'avocado' comes from the misspelling of the original 'aguacate' of the Spaniards. This fruit is the only one that is rich in both proteins and oil at the same time. It is also rich in Vitamin A, with moderate amounts of B and C. In Cuba it is mainly eaten as a salad, in slices with salt and vinegar. The pulp can be directly applied to the skin and hair to prevent dryness.

Aguacate Cimarrón

Dendrocereus nudiflorus (Engelm.) Britton & Rose

Family: Cactaceae

Origin: Cuba, endemic.

Height: Up to 7 m (23 ft) when very old.

Trunk: Massive (up to 1 m or 3¼ ft in diameter in very old trees), cylindrical, light brown.

Canopy: A tree-like cactus, with hanging branches.

Leaves: Leafless; the branches are green and succulent, with three to five ribs bearing the rigid spines that grow in woolly dots along the edge of the ribs in the branches.

Flowers: Solitary, large, cup-like, with many white petals tinged pink inside and white to light pink stamens.

Fruit: A large fleshy fruit, elliptical, containing numerous small black seeds.

Comments: This cactus used to be common in Cuban coastal scrublands and forests. Today it is threatened with extinction. Beautiful individual examples can be seen on the Varadero peninsula on the northern coast of Matanzas. The popular name stems from the similarity between the fruit of this plant and that of the Avocado ('Aguacate' in Spanish).

Aguedita

(Quina del País, Quina de la Tierra, Bitter Bush)

Picramnia pentandra Sw.

Family: Picramniaceae (Simaroubaceae)

Origin: West Indies, Florida (USA), Bahamas, north of South America.

Height: Up to 10 m (33 ft), usually less, achieving the height of a small tree or shrub.

Trunk: Slender, branching, with smooth, grey bark.

Canopy: Rounded and dense.

Leaves: Growing alternately from the twigs, made up of 5 to 13 leaflets of elliptical form, 5–13 cm (2–5 in) long with very sharp tips; brilliant green with a bluish caste.

Flowers: Very small, in panicles 7–20 cm (about 3–8 in) long, with five spear-shaped, white petals and five stamens. Blooms all year round.

Fruit: Berries arranged in a drooping raceme, red when unripe, becoming almost black as they ripen.

Comments: This is a shrub or small tree commonly appearing in the undergrowth of semi-deciduous forests. The ripe fruits droop down to touch the soil but no animals touch them because, it is thought, of their bitter taste. During the nineteenth century wars of Cuban independence the leaves and bark of Aguedita were used by physicians for the relief of malarial fever, hence the popular Cuban name 'Quina del País'.

Alamo de la India

(Sacred Fig)
Ficus religiosa L.

Family: Moraceae

Origin: India.

Height: Up to 35 m (115 ft), usually less in Cuba.

Trunk: Straight, with some aerial roots.

Canopy: Rounded, deciduous.

Leaves: Alternate, heart-shaped, with elongated pointed tips. They are glossy-green, and move with the slightest breeze because of their long petioles. The entire leaf is about 25–30 cm (10–12 in) long.

Flowers: As with all members of the genus *Ficus*, the flowers of this tree are contained inside a round structure (1 cm or about ½ in diameter) called a receptacle, which in this case is purple in colour. Blossoms almost all year round.

Fruit: This tree does not produce fruits due to the lack of a pollinator insect. Reproduces asexually.

Comments: This is a commonly used tree in parks, streets and open spaces. Its strong growth occasionally causes damage to pavements and its roots can play havoc with plumbing systems. Its species name, *religiosa*, is based on its being a sacred tree in India and Sri Lanka, where it is forbidden to harm it or to use its timber. Alamo de la India is common in the Havana neighbourhoods of La Víbora, Vedado and Playa.

Algarrobo

(Algarrobo del País, Saman)
Samanea saman (Jacq.) Merr.

Family: Mimosaceae (Leguminosae)

Origin: Tropical America, naturalized in Cuba.

Height: Up to 25 m (80 ft).

Trunk: Up to 2 m (6½ ft) in diameter and extremely tall, the lower half being straight and without branches, the upper half with numerous branches. The bark is brown, rough and furrowed.

Canopy: Widely extended, like an enormous umbrella.

Leaves: Compound, with many bright green leaflets 2–8 cm (¾–3 in) long.

Flowers: In the axils of leaves, with a stalk 10–12 cm (4–5 in) long, in globular clusters. The blossoms, which appear in the rainy season, have long pink and white stamens.

Fruit: Flat, bean-like pods 10–20 cm (4–8 in) long, with small brown seeds.

These seed pods appear during the dry winter season.

Comments: These beautiful perennials are among the tallest trees in Cuba; frequently found beside old roads where they were planted for shade, they are also planted for ornamental purposes. Algarrobos are abundant in pastures, where the cows much appreciate the fallen leaves and seed pods, which are considered by country people to improve the quality of the cows' milk. The reddish-brown wood is used for making furniture. The leaves, as in other legumes, close on cloudy days and at night.

Algarrobo de Olor

(Aroma Francesa, Lengua de Mujer, Músico, Mother-in-Law's Tongue)
Albizia lebbek (L.) Benth.

Synonym: *Mimosa lebbek* L.

Family: Mimosaceae (Leguminosae)

Origin: Tropics of Asia, Africa and Australia. Cultivated in all tropical regions of the world. In Cuba, after initial cultivation, it now grows spontaneously in the wild.

Height: Up to 15 m (50 ft), often less.

Trunk: Straight, grey, quite smooth, up to 40 cm (16 in) diameter. The twigs, which grow from the branches, have a furry surface.

Canopy: In the shape of an umbrella.

Leaves: Compound, with light green asymmetrical oblong leaflets measuring 2–4 cm (¾–1½ in) long. The petiole is between 2 and 10 cm (¾ and 4 in) long and has a round gland at its base.

Flowers: Tiny, grouped in small globular clusters, with long, greenish-yellow stamens. Strongly scented.

Fruit: Flat seed pods, yellow ochre coloured when dry, measuring about 15 cm (6 in) long, which contain up to ten flat brown seeds. When the wind blows, the seed pods make a whispering sound.

Comments: This is a very common tree in Cuba. It was initially planted to provide shade beside roads, from where it seeded itself to neighbouring fields. It is widely used to provide shade on coffee plantations. The wood is used for making furniture and, in the countryside, for construction. The sound produced by the dry seed pods when blown by the wind is the cause of the tree's popular names: 'Músico' (musician) and 'Lengua de Mujer' (woman's tongue).

Almácigo

(Almácigo Azucarero, Almácigo Colorado, Gumbo-Limbo, West Indian Birch, Naked Indian)
Bursera simarouba (L.) Sargent

Family: Burseraceae

Origin: Tropical America.

Height: Up to 20 m (65 ft), usually less in Cuba.

Trunk: Straight, with smooth, shiny, coppery-red bark that peels away from the trunk in papery strips. The trunk can reach a diameter of 1 m (3¼ ft) in very old trees.

Canopy: Rounded, variably leafy, deciduous.

Leaves: Alternate, made up of five to nine glossy-green leaflets of variable shape, about 3–8 cm (1–3 in) long, with pointed tips. The entire leaf is 10–20 cm (4–8 in) long.

Flowers: Small, numerous, growing in panicles; the flowers are greenish-white and fragrant. Blossoms May to June.

Fruit: A triangular dark red seed pod 5–10 mm (¼–½ in) in size, containing one or two seeds.

Comments: Almácigo is one of Cuba's commonest trees, growing in semi-deciduous and dry coastal forests. It is used as an ornamental plant because of its beautiful coppery-red trunk. It is also renowned for its medicinal properties, being used as a cure for conditions of the chest and stomach. Almácigo is used for creating hedges around fields, as lengths of branch cut from the tree take root very quickly.

Almendra

(Almendro de la India, Tropical Almond, Almond Tree, West Indian Almond)
Terminalia catappa L.

Family: Combretaceae

Origin: Southeast Asia, northern Australia and the Pacific islands.

Height: 5–16 m (16–52 ft), occasionally taller.

Trunk: Straight and thick, with smooth, light brown bark.

Canopy: A rounded crown formed by widely spreading branches disposed in almost horizontal whorls; deciduous.

Leaves: Very large, alternate, leathery, obovate with rounded tips, upwards of 30 cm (12 in) long and 16 cm (6 in) wide. They are shiny dark green above, paler below, and turn bright red before falling from the tree.

Flowers: The small, white, inconspicuous flowers appear in narrow axillary racemes up to 25 cm (10 in) long.

Fruit: Oval, yellow when ripe, slightly fleshy outside and hard and fibrous inside, containing a single seed.

Comments: This beautiful tree, although not native to Cuba, is often seen in parks and alongside urban avenues, as well as beside beaches. Children often use stones to crush the fibrous outer shell of the fruit in order to extract and eat the central nut. The fruit floats in both fresh and salt water, which is probably why the species has spread over such great distances. Almendra withstands drought and salt winds, and is thus used for ornamental planting along the seashore.

Anacagüita

Sterculia apetala (Jacq.) H. Karst.

Family: Malvaceae (formerly Sterculiaceae)

Origin: Tropical America.

Height: Up to 30 m (100 ft).

Trunk: Very large: About 80–100 cm (32–40 in) diameter, with tabular roots and brown bark.

Canopy: Extended.

Leaves: Up to 50 cm (20 in) long, heart-shaped; dull green, their lower surface being covered with fine wool. The leaves fall from the tree in the dry season.

Flowers: Small, grouped in panicles; the petals are yellow with purple spots. The tree flowers during the dry season.

Fruit: Seed pods about 15 cm (6 in) wide. They have a hairy outer surface

that divides into five parts when opened showing the oval, greyish seeds of about 2 cm (¾ in) diameter.

Comments: Anacagüita is a naturalized tree that mostly occurs in the inhabited areas of eastern Cuba. The seeds are often eaten toasted.

Araucaria

(Siete Pisos, Palma Estrella, Arbol de Navidad, Norfolk Island Pine)
Araucaria heterophylla (Salisb.) Franco

Synonym: *Araucaria excelsa* auct. non R. Br.

Family: Araucariaceae

Origin: Norfolk Islands.

Height: 20–25 m (65–80 ft).

Trunk: Straight, sparsely branched, with coarse dark brown to black bark.

Canopy: An evergreen tree with a conical canopy of branches arranged in layers.

Leaves: Small, dark green, less than 1 cm (about ½ in) long; scaly; overlapping, clothing all the branches.

Flowers: This plant, as all gymnosperms, does not produce true flowers; the reproductive structures are similar to cones, the male cone being smaller than the female one.

Fruit: The tree does not produce true fruits; the triangular, winged seeds are contained in the rounded, woody, female cone.

Comments: This is a common ornamental tree, widely planted in public and domestic gardens, where it is occasionally decorated for Christmas. Araucaria thrives near the sea, and is commonly used for ornamental purposes along the coast.

Arbol de las Salchichas

(Sausage Tree)
Kigelia pinnata DC.

Synonym: *Kigelia africana* (Lam.) Benth.

Family: Bignoniaceae

Origin: Tropical East Africa.

Height: Up to 15 m (50 ft).

Trunk: Straight, with rough, greyish-brown bark.

Canopy: Extended, with spreading branches; perennial

Leaves: Alternate, large compound leaves with five to seven leaflets, very rough-textured, dull green, measuring about 30–40 cm (12–16 in) long.

Flowers: Very attractive, hanging in racemes up to 3 m (10 ft) long. The flowers are cup-shaped, large, yellow ochre outside and dark reddish-brown inside. Their strong smell attracts bats, which pollinate the tree. The flowers open at night and fall in the morning if they have been pollinated. The tree blossoms several times per year.

Fruit: The fruits look like very large, hard, heavy, light brown sausages up to 50 cm (20 in) long and 20 cm (8 in) in

diameter, hanging from long stalks. They contain a creamy-white pulp in which are embedded numerous seeds.

Comments: Despite its name, the fruit of this tree is not edible and, because of its considerable weight (5 kg [11 lb]) can be very harmful if it falls from the tree onto a luckless passer-by. In East Africa these fruits are considered sacred and are used in traditional medicine.

Arbol del Nim

(Nim, Neem, Nim Tree)
Azadirachta indica A. Juss.

WARNING: The fruit is poisonous.

Family: Meliaceae

Origin: Southeast Asia.

Height: Up to 15 m (50 ft), usually less.

Trunk: Straight, with rough, light brown bark.

Canopy: Rounded, densely leafed, perennial.

Leaves: Alternate, compound, consisting of pairs of dull green leaflets with minutely toothed borders, the whole leaf is 20–25 cm (8–10 in) long.

Flowers: Small, appearing in lacy axillary panicles, light lilac-violet and fragrant. The tree blossoms in the rainy season.

Fruit: Berry-like, oily, yellow-golden fruit about 10–15 mm (½ in) long, containing a very hard seed.

Comments: In Cuba, the Nim Tree has only recently become popular. It has, however, been cultivated for thousands of years, mainly in sub-Saharan Africa and in the Middle East, because it provides excellent shade and food for horses and camels. Bees often visit its flowers, and bats and birds feed on the golden-yellow fruits. In Cuba an insecticide oil is extracted from its seeds and it is planted for this purpose in many urban agricultural plots. The Nim Tree is closely related to Paraíso (*Melia azederach*).

Arbol del Pan

(Fruta de Pan, Mapén, Breadfruit)
Artocarpus altilis (S. Parkinson) Fosberg

Synonym: *Artocarpus communis* J.R. & G. Forst.

Family: Moraceae

Origin: Islands of the South Pacific.

Height: 15–20 m (50–65 ft), but commonly less.

Trunk: Straight; the bark is smooth and greyish with spots of lichen. The branches break easily.

Canopy: Rounded, with distinctively shaped leaves.

Leaves: Alternate, very large with seven deep lobes of which the central lobe is the largest. Each lobe has a very sharp tip. The leaves are deep green above and paler beneath, with prominent veins. The entire leaf can measure up to 60 cm (24 in) long and 40–50 cm (16–20 in) wide.

Flowers: The tiny female flowers form a round, prickly ball 20–30 cm (8–12 in) in diameter, sprouting on a stalk from the branch. The male flowers are very small and form a yellow catkin 30 cm (12 in) long. Blooms all year round, mainly in the rainy season.

Fruit: Greenish-yellow, prickly spheres about 30 cm (12 in) in diameter. The majority of the varieties are seedless, containing a creamy-white pulp. When seeds are present, they are rounded, brown and about 3 cm (1 in) diameter, and they germinate very rapidly inside the fallen fruit.

Comments: The carbohydrate and vitamin-rich fruit of this interesting tree has been eaten by the Polynesian people for thousands of years. It was first introduced from Tahití to the island of St Vincent in the West Indies in 1793, by Captain Bligh in the ship *Providence*, in order to provide food for African slaves. Since that time the tree has spread throughout the Caribbean. In Cuba it is frequently found in the Eastern provinces, where fruit of the seedless variety called Mapén is eaten baked or boiled.

Arbol del Viajero

(Traveller's Tree, Traveller's Palm)
Ravenala madagascariensis F.F. Gmel.

Family: Strelitziaceae

Origin: Endemic to Madagascar.

Height: Can grow to 7–8 m (23–26 ft), but is generally shorter in Cuba.

Trunk: Straight, woody, without branches, terminating in a crown of large upright leaves. Each plant may bear several stems, growing in clumps.

Canopy: A terminal fan-like crown of large leaves.

Leaves: Very large, with long petioles and blades 1–2 m (3¼–6½ ft) long. The leaves are similar to those of the banana tree, growing vertically in the shape of a giant fan, with the dead leaves remaining attached to the trunk for a long time. The leaf has a hollow sheath at its base, which envelops the trunk, forming a cavity that can contain large quantities of rainwater. Passers-by may drink this liquid by making a hole in the side of the natural container, hence the name 'Traveller's Palm'.

Flowers: The flowers appear in very large inflorescences emerging from the axils of the leaves; they are composed of a dozen long, triangular bracts which grow alternately from the stem and upon which are supported large numbers of white flowers.

Fruit: The seed pod contains a triple cavity in which are housed several seeds wrapped in a blue membrane. The tree can also be propagated from the new suckers that grow at its base.

Comments: The water held in the leaf sheaths may safely be drunk; the quantity can reach more than 1 litre (about 2 pints). In Madagascar, the wood of the trunk is used for construction and the leaves for thatch. In Cuba, the tree is commonly planted in parks and gardens because of its attractive appearance.

Bacona

(Jaimiquí)
Albizia cubana Britton & Wilson

Family: Mimosaceae (Leguminosae)

Origin: Cuba, endemic.

Height: Up to 15 m (50 ft).

Trunk: Straight, thick, with smooth, light brown bark.

Canopy: Rounded, leafy, perennial.

Leaves: Alternate, compound, divided into three to four pairs of pinnae made up of many small, bright green leaflets. The entire leaf is 5–10 cm (2–4 in) long.

Flowers: From March to June bunches of tiny creamy-white flowers appear on the tree. They have with five sepals, five petals and numerous brush-like stamens, and measure 5–7 mm (about ¼ in) across.

Fruit: The oblong, light brown, flat, furry seed pod is 8–20 cm (3–8 in) long and 2–4 cm (¾–1½ in) wide, and contains elliptical brown seeds.

Comments: The Indian name Bacona is derived from the place of the same name, which is a Biosphere Reserve in Santiago de Cuba province. This huge tree has very hard wood that is used for posts, railway sleepers and in rural construction and carpentry. Bacona grows naturally in coastal woods in the Eastern provinces of the island.

Bagá

(Palo Bobo, Guanábana Cimarrona, Pond Apple)
Annona glabra L.

Synonym: *Annona palustris* L.

Family: Annonaceae

Origin: North of South America, Antilles and West Africa.

Height: 2–9 m (6½–30 ft)

Trunk: Conical, broad at the base and narrow at the top, greyish-black, smooth.

Canopy: Comparatively small, composed of scarce, short branches.

Leaves: About 15 cm (6 in) long, elliptical with a round base and a pointed tip, deep lustrous green, deciduous.

Flowers: Single flowers about 3 cm (1 in) wide, the three outer petals being creamy-white with a crimson red spot at the base, the inner ones white at the edge and deep red at the centre. Strongly scented. Flowers April to June.

Fruit: Round, smooth, yellow when ripe, about 12 cm (5 in) long. The seeds are brown.

Comments: The Bagá tree is common in marshy areas near the coast, in swampy forests inland, and at river mouths. It is a common tree in the Ciénaga de Zapata Biosphere Reserve (in Matanzas province) and in the Parque del Bagá on the northeastern coast of the island. The fruit is eaten by cattle. Dried branches of this tree are often used in flower arrangements.

Bienvestido

(Bien Vestida, Amor y Celos, Piñón Florido, Piñón Amoroso, Mata-ratón, Quick Stick, Pea Tree)
Gliricidia sepium (Jacq.) Kunth ex Walp.

WARNING: Both the roots and the bark are extremely poisonous.

Family: Fabaceae (Leguminosae)

Origin: Tropical America.

Height: A small tree growing up to 10 m (33 ft), although in Cuba it seldom achieves this height.

Trunk: Stout in very old trees, profusely branched, with greyish-brown bark.

Canopy: Deciduous; rounded, open canopy.

Leaves: Alternate, compound, with 7 to 17 ovate to spear-shaped leaflets 3–7 cm (1–2¾ in) long and 2–3 cm (¾–1 in) wide, with pointed tips; light green, deciduous during the winter (December to March).

Flowers: Appear in axillary clusters about 15 cm (6 cm) long of numerous pinkish-mauve to white blossoms 1.5–2 cm (½–¾ in) wide, with corollas of five petals. The tree blooms to very decorative effect in March, before its leaves have appeared.

Fruit: Bienvestido produces a bean-like seed pod 10–15 cm (4–6 in) long and 1.5 cm (½ in) wide. However, the tree rarely fruits in Cuba and it is mainly propagated by large cuttings, which root rapidly.

Comments: 'Bien vestido' translates into English as 'well-dressed', an appropriate name for a tree that produces a

glorious show of flowers somewhat resembling cherry blossom, but which only last for a few days. The tree is planted for shade on coffee plantations and is also used to create hedges on cattle farms. The termite-proof wood is often used for furniture and the leaves are fed to cattle. The honey produced by bees that visit Bienvestido trees is especially delicious.

Bija

(Achiote)
Bixa orellana L.

Family: Bixaceae

Origin: Tropical America.

Height: Up to 4 m (13 ft).

Trunk: Branching from the base.

Canopy: Flattened.

Leaves: Perennial, alternate, ovate to heart-shaped with sharp tips and long petioles; deep green, about 20 cm (8 in) long and 4–15 cm (1½–6 in) wide.

Flowers: Very attractive in terminal clusters, with five pink overlapping petals, twisted in the bud, and numerous stamens. Flowers from June to November.

Fruit: The red seed pods are 3–4 cm (1–1½ in) long and wide with rough outer surfaces; they open as two valves revealing numerous red, angular seeds.

Comments: Bija is a pre-Columbian plant that is thought to have been brought to Cuba by the Arawak Indians. They used the orange dye contained in its seeds to paint their bodies for religious ceremonies and for protection against bites and stings from mosquitoes and other insects. The dye obtained from Bija is still widely used in Cuban traditional cooking to add a 'saffron' tinge to rice and meat. There is a garden variety with bright red seed pods.

Cacao

(Cocoa, Chocolate Tree)
Theobroma cacao L.

Family: Malvaceae (formerly Sterculiaceae)

Origin: Central and South America.

Height: Up to 8 m (26 ft).

Trunk: Smooth, brown, the flowers growing directly from the bark; about 25 cm (10 in) diameter.

Canopy: Branching, not thickly leaved.

Leaves: Large, simple ellipses 15–30 cm (6–12 in) long, with sharp tips. The mature leaves are deep green, the young ones very soft and of a pale pink colour. Cacao is perennial.

Flowers: The scented white flowers appear in inconspicuous bunches growing directly from the branches.

Fruit: Large ovate fruits about 25 cm (10 in) long, ridged, rough and pointed, with five cavities inside containing numerous rounded seeds. The pods are initially green, becoming yellow or red at maturity.

Comments: Cacao is economically important in Cuba and many other countries. The Latin name *Theobroma* means 'Food for the Gods', referring to the chocolate produced from the ground and roasted seeds. The Aztecs in Mexico were the first people to make a drink from Cacao seeds, which they offered to their gods. They added vanilla (a flavouring produced from the seeds of an orchid) to enhance the flavour. Cuba is an exporter of Cacao. The main plantations are in Baracoa, in the easternmost part of the island.

Calistemon

(Palo Basigato, Falso Sauce, Bottlebrush Tree)
Callistemon speciosus (Sims) Sweet

Family: Myrtaceae

Origin: Australia.

Height: Up to 3–4 m (10–13 ft)

Trunk: Leaning and profusely branched.

Canopy: A cascade of weeping branches.

Leaves: Alternate, small, rough, spear-shaped with pointed tips, slightly hairy, light green.

Flowers: The inflorescences at the ends of the branches contain numerous flowers arranged close to one another around the stem. The flowers have a tiny calyx and corolla, with long red stamens and style, each one having the appearance of a diminutive feather-duster, while the whole inflorescence looks like a red bottlebrush. Blossoms from March to April.

Fruit: A small, brown, cylindrical seed pod with three to four cavities containing the powder-like seeds that are dispersed by the wind when the fruit is dry.

Comments: This beautiful tree is often used as an ornamental in parks and avenues, and is sometimes confused with the willow because of its weeping branches. Closely related species also used for ornamental purposes are *Callistemon citrinus*, *C. hortensis* and *C. lanceolatus*. Bees frequently visit Calistemon trees, for their flowers are particularly abundant in nectar.

Cañafístola

(Caña Fistula, Shower of Gold, Indian Laburnum)
Cassia fistula L.

Family: Caesalpiniaceae (Leguminosae)

Origin: Tropical Asia.

Height: A small tree 7–8 m (23–26 ft) tall.

Trunk: Straight, with smooth brown bark.

Canopy: Narrow, deciduous.

Leaves: Alternate, compound, very large (up to 50 cm [20 in] long) with four to eight pairs of leaflets 10–12 cm (4–6 in) long, bright green above and silvery below.

Flowers: Very showy, in large, cascading racemes 30–50 cm (12–20 in) long, each containing up to 30 golden yellow flowers of five petals suspended from a small stalk. The plant flowers from May to August.

Fruit: The long, pendant, cylindrical brown pod about 40 cm (16 in) long and 2–3 cm (¾–1 in) in diameter contains numerous flat seeds surrounded by a sweet brown pulp; they take over a year to ripen.

Comments: Cañafístola is one of the most beautiful exotic flowering trees and is used extensively throughout the island of Cuba in streets and parks. The pulp in the seed pods is used as a laxative; Cañafístola was one of the earliest medicinal plants to be introduced into the island.

Cañandonga

(Cañafístula Cimarrona, Coral Shower, Horse Cassia)
Cassia grandis L.f.

Family: Caesalpiniaceae (Leguminosae)

Origin: Eastern Cuba; Central and South America.

Height: A tall tree growing to 15–30 m (50–100 ft).

Trunk: Straight, smooth, up to 1 m (3¼ ft) diameter in very old trees; the bark is grey.

Canopy: Deciduous, the canopy appearing rounded to extended.

Leaves: Alternate, compound with 8 to 20 pairs of leaflets 3–5 cm (1–2 in) wide and 10–15 cm (4–6 in) long; deep green.

Flowers: Very decorative; the coral pink to red flowers have six rounded petals 15 mm (½ in) wide, with long, golden yellow stamens; they appear in dense axillary clusters 10–20 cm (4–8 in) long. Flowers briefly and spectacularly at the beginning of the rainy season (May–June).

Fruit: Cylindrical, brown, rough seed pods 30–90 cm (12–36 in) long, containing numerous flat seeds, arranged like stacks of coins in individual compartments, embedded in an evil-smelling (but delicious) brown pulp.

Comments: There is some debate as to whether Cañandonga is indigenous or naturalized, but it is very common in the Eastern provinces of Cuba. It occurs naturally in semi-deciduous forests, and is cultivated in gardens and open spaces for its dramatically beautiful blossom. The pulp is used for making refreshing drinks and has medicinal properties: it is a laxative and also increases the haemoglobin level of the blood.

Caoba

(Caoba de Cuba, Caoba Antillana, Mahogany)
Swietenia mahagoni (L.) Jacq.

Family: Meliaceae

Origin: Caribbean islands.

Height: Up to 20 m (65 ft).

Trunk: Straight with deep brown, furrowed bark; it can reach about 2 m (6½ ft) in diameter when growing in deep soil.

Canopy: Round, dense foliage.

Leaves: Compound with two to five pairs of leaflets asymmetric at their base; vivid green, 3–7 cm (1–2¾ in) long; the whole leaf is up to 30 cm (12 in) long; deciduous in the dry season.

Flowers: Inconspicuous white flowers in inflorescences. The tree flowers at the beginning of the rainy season.

Fruit: Brown, woody seed pods 6–10 cm (2¼–4 in) long containing numerous seeds attached to reddish-brown papery wings, which permit their dispersal in the wind. The fruits ripen in February/March, when the tree is without its leaves.

Comments: Caoba is one of the most outstanding timber trees in Cuba, famous for its hardiness and beautiful colour. Having been harvested for over five centuries, it has become scarce on the island. Caoba trees can grow in most Cuban soil types, with the exception of particularly poor ones. Outstandingly good Caoba furniture may be seen in the Museum of Colonial Art in Havana's Cathedral Square. Recently, *Swietenia macrophylla*, a species related to Caoba, has been introduced to the island. It is known as Caoba de Honduras, has larger leaves and seeds, and can hybridize with the native species, producing an excellent and fast-growing timber tree.

Carambola

(Ciruela China, Ciruelón Chino, Star Fruit)
Averhoa carambola L.

Family: Oxalidaceae

Origin: Tropical Asia.

Height: Up to 10 m (33 ft) but often less in Cuba.

Trunk: Smooth, brown trunk with numerous branches.

Canopy: Rounded, densely leafed, perennial.

Leaves: Alternate, growing in a spiral pattern direct from the branches, compound, with five to ten oval leaflets. The leaves are deep glossy green and measure 15–20 cm (6–8 in) long.

Flowers: Small but very attractive, the reddish-purple flowers grow in clusters on the trunk and branches. The tree blossoms several times a year.

Fruit: The waxy, fragrant fruit with five deep ribs turns orange-yellow when ripe. It is elliptical in form, 10–12 cm (4–5 in) long, and when cut sideways produces star-shaped slices. Each rib of the fruit contains several seeds.

Comments: This beautiful tree may be planted both as an ornamental and as a useful fruit tree. Its dense foliage contrasted with its golden fruits is very attractive. The flesh of the fruit is initially sour, but is very sweet when it ripens. Carambola fruit is rich in Vitamin C; delicious juice is extracted from it and the fruit is used for puddings, in salads and for making wine.

Cardenal

(Arbol Cardenal, Pride of Guatemala)
Phyllocarpus septentrionalis Donn. Smith

Family: Caesalpiniaceae (Leguminosae)

Origin: Guatemala and Honduras.

Height: A tall tree growing up to 20 m (65 ft).

Trunk: Straight, smooth, with light brown bark.

Canopy: Deciduous, extended, with arching branches.

Leaves: Alternate, compound of leaflets about 8 cm (3 in) long and 5 cm (2 in) wide, arranged in four to eight pairs, bright green.

Flowers: The spectacular blooms consist of dense clusters of tiny bright red flowers with six petals and very long, red stamens. Flowers in the dry season (February–March).

Fruit: Dehiscent flat seed pods of about 15 cm (6 in) long and 5 cm (2 in) wide, with winged seeds.

Comments: This is one of the island's most beautiful trees, although it is not very common. One group that merits inspection is established at the National Botanic Garden, in the Central America zone.

Carolina

(Shaving Brush Tree)
Pseudobombax ellipticum (Kunth) Dugand

Synonym: *Bombax ellipticum* Kunth

Family: Malvaceae (formerly Bombacaceae)

Origin: Mexico, Central America.

Height: Up to 10 m (33 ft).

Trunk: Becomes extremely wide when the tree is old, apart from when it is propagated asexually from the branches. The main trunk is cylindrical, green to greyish-green, with branches extending from its lower parts.

Canopy: Extended, the direction of branch growth inclining towards the horizontal.

Leaves: A finger-like, partially folded compound of five to six leaflets measuring 5–30 cm (2–12 in) long and 4–17 cm (1½–6¾ in) wide, distributed at the end of the branches; vivid green. New leaves are bright red, forming a spectacular contrast with the tree's green trunk.

Flowers: Appearing in pairs or singly at the end of the branches, they look like shaving brushes, having numerous long, brilliant pink or white stamens. The corolla has five dark or light pink petals, which curl when the flower is open. The flower, which is approximately 15 cm (6 in) long, appears from February to April during the dry season when the tree is without leaves.

Fruit: Not commonly produced by Carolina trees growing in Cuba, probably due to the lack of a pollinating insect.

Comments: A spectacular tree, from which the flowers fall to form a pink or white carpet. Commonly used in landscape gardening for the beauty of its trunk, leaves and flowers and its tolerance of poorly irrigated soil.

Casia Nodosa

(Casia de Java, Apple Blossom Cassia, Nodding Cassia)
Cassia javanica L.

Synonym: *Cassia nodosa* Buch.-Ham. ex Roxb.

Family: Caesalpiniaceae (Leguminosae)

Origin: Southeast Asia.

Height: Can grow to about 30 m (100 ft), but is much shorter in Cuba.

Trunk: Straight, with numerous knotted branches and light brown bark.

Canopy: Deciduous, extended, with dense foliage.

Leaves: Alternate, compound, with numerous dark green leaflets.

Flowers: Highly showy, appearing in dense clusters; the flowers are pink fading to near-white, which gives them a variegated appearance. Each flower has five petals with long curved stamens, and a subtle scent of apples. Blooms from April to June, before the new leaves appear.

Fruit: A long, cylindrical, brown seed pod about 20–30 cm (8–10 in) in length, with numerous flat seeds stacked up like piles of small coins.

Comments: This is a highly attractive tree, widely cultivated in tropical countries. It was introduced into Cuba during the first half of the twentieth century and is now grown in numerous public spaces. An outstanding group may be seen in the Japanese Garden of the National Botanic Garden, where it was planted instead of the Cherry, which would not have survived in the tropical heat. Its delicious scent and showy flowers are a worthy addition to the garden.

Casuarina

(Pino de Australia, Australian Pine)
Casuarina equisetifolia Forst.

Family: Casuarinaceae

Origin: Australia.

Height: Up to 20 m (65 ft), usually less in Cuba.

Trunk: Straight, slender, with long thin branches. The bark is brown and scaly; the tree has tabular roots.

Canopy: Varied in shape, with thin, drooping twigs.

Leaves: Although leafless, or at first sight appearing to have pine needles, this tree actually has very peculiar, minute (3–4 mm [less than ²⁄₁₀ in]), greyish-green scaly leaves.

Flowers: The sexes are separated in different flowers on the same tree. The male flowers are thin cylindrical spikes with visible stamens. The female ones are contained within a green, cone-like, woody structure about 2 cm (¾ in) long and 1.5 cm (½ in) wide. Flowers in April to May.

Fruit: Very small winged seeds are contained in a brown cone-like structure.

Comments: This tree is very common (rather more common than is desired) all over the country. It was introduced as an ornamental and as a fast-growing tree to provide windbreaks. It was also used for fixing the sand dunes next to beaches, but it contaminated the sand and has now been removed from the majority of Cuban beaches. Casuarina is an aggressive

competitor in natural ecosystems because it is a fast-growing tree with easily sprouting seeds, and tends to overtake slow-growing native trees. It owes its local name, 'Pino de Australia', to the false 'pine needles' resembling those of real pines.

Cedro

(Cedro Hembra, Cedar)
Cedrela odorata L.

Synonym: *Cederla mexicana* M. Roemer

Family: Meliaceae

Origin: Tropical America.

Height: Up to 20 m (65 ft), occasionally taller.

Trunk: Straight; greyish, smooth, 80–100 cm (32–40 in) in diameter.

Canopy: Round, with dense foliage.

Leaves: Compound, with many leaflets 3–6 cm (1–2¼ in) long, irregular at their base; opaque green on both sides, with a disagreeable odour. The leaves fall from the tree during the dry season.

Flowers: Inconspicuous, grouped in tiny bunches.

Fruit: The brown woody seed pods, about 4 cm (1½ in) long, contain numerous seeds with papery wings which facilitate their dispersal.

Comments: Cedro has become comparatively rare in Cuba, due to its wood having been harvested for five centuries. It occurs naturally in original forest areas, as well as in managed woods. Its soft, porous timber is used for making furniture and cigar boxes and has insect-repelling properties. The related species *Cedrela cubensis*, commonly known as 'Cedro Macho', is endemic to Cuba, occurring in dry forests. Its leaflets differ from the classic Cedro in that their lower surfaces are light green and their seed pods are smaller than those of *Cedrela odorata*.

Ceiba

(Kapok, Ceibo, Seiba)
Ceiba pentandra (L.) Gaertn.

WARNING: Large, sharp spines grow from the young trunk and branches.

Family: Malvaceae (formerly Bombacaceae)

Origin: Tropics of America and Africa.

Height: Up to 40 m (130 ft).

Trunk: Extremely wide (up to 2 m or 6½ ft in diameter), with roots growing in the form of vertical walls which anchor the trunk to the soil. The bark is greyish, and scattered with stiff black spines on the young trunk and branches.

Canopy: Extended.

Leaves: Similar to the extended fingers of a hand, composed of five to eight light green leaflets 10–20 cm (4–8 in) long. The leaves fall from the tree during the dry season.

Flowers: Appear in groups of three or four at the ends of the branches; they have corollas formed of five petals whose outside surface is woolly while the internal surface is cream and pink; 3–4 cm (1–1½ in) long. The flower blooms in the dry season, but not annually.

Fruit: Brownish, woody seed pods 12–16 cm (4¾–6¼ in) long, filled with greyish wool and numerous small, round seeds, which are dispersed by the wind.

Comments: Ceiba trees often stand as the last remnants of the Cuban forests that were cleared during the nineteenth century for grazing or for the planting of sugar. One often sees them when travelling in the interior of the island. The Ceiba is considered an extremely holy tree by practitioners of Afro-Cuban religions. Its 'wool' is used for filling pillows and mattresses. Many Cuban cities possess outstanding examples of Ceiba trees, and in Havana a celebrated Ceiba stands on the site of the foundation of the city, near a column erected in 1754 to commemorate the original tree. The Ceiba in Havana's Fraternity Park was planted on 24 February 1928, its roots being surrounded by soil brought from historic places in the 21 countries that make up the Americas.

Ceibon

(Drago, Seibón)
Bombacopsis cubensis A. Robyns

Family: Malvaceae (formerly Bombacaceae)

Origin: Cuba, endemic to the karst mountains of western Cuba ('mogotes').

Height: 10–15 m (33–50 ft).

Trunk: Curved at the base where it emerges from the vertical rocky slopes of the 'mogotes'; wide at the bottom, becoming more slender towards the top. Green, 20–50 cm (8–20 in) diameter.

Canopy: Scarce branches, growing in a vertical direction.

Leaves: Similar to the extended fingers of a hand, with five to nine leaflets of up to 10 cm (4 in) in length; pale green; few leaves at the ends of the branches. The leaves fall during the dry season.

Flowers: Shaped like a shaving-brush with a cup-shaped calyx and numerous stamens with reddish filaments; about 12 cm (5 in) long. The tree flowers during the dry season, after its leaves have fallen.

Fruit: Brownish seed pods, full of small seeds and yellowish wool; 6–7 cm (2¼–2¾ in) long, 3–3.5 cm (1–1¼ in) wide.

Comments: This peculiar but beautiful tree only grows on the vertical slopes of Cuba's celebrated 'mogotes', never occurring spontaneously in flat conditions. It is rarely cultivated (although a few specimens may be seen at the National Botanic Garden), but even when artificially propagated the tree conserves its natural curved base. It may be seen growing on the 'mogotes' of Pinar del Río, in Havana province and on the Isla de la Juventud.

Cheflera

(Umbrella Tree, Octopus Tree)
Brassaia actinophylla Endl.

Synonym: *Schefflera actinophylla* (Endl.) Harms.

Family: Araliaceae

Origin: New Guinea, Australia.

Height: Up to 10 m (33 ft), less in Cuba.

Trunk: Commonly multiple, vertical, branchless; the bark is pale greyish-brown.

Canopy: Formed by many umbrella-shaped crowns of leaves.

Leaves: Very large, growing alternately from the trunk, with stalks 50–80 cm (20–32 in) long, made up of seven to ten leaflets with long stalks forming a large umbrella shape; each leaflet has a 10–12 cm (4–5 in) stalk and is roughly oblong, 30–40 cm (12–16 in) long with a very sharp tip, undulating edges and a yellow central vein. The leaflets are dark shiny green above and paler below, with a prominent central vein. When the leaves fall they leave triangular scars on the trunk.

Flowers: The small, vermilion flowers grow in rounded clusters from the ribs (five to eight in number, measuring 70–80 cm [28–32 in] long) of the inverted umbrella-shaped inflorescences at the end of the branches.

Fruit: Very small crimson berries. The tree is also propagated from cuttings.

Comments: Cheflera is a spectacular ornamental tree often planted in gardens and beside buildings, where its brilliant umbrellas of leaves and enormous inflorescences, looking rather like large red octopuses, are seen to maximum effect.

Cigua

(Lancewood, Capberry Sweetwood, Sweet Torchwood)
Nectandra coriacea (Sw.) Griseb.

Family: Lauraceae

Origin: West Indies, Florida (USA) and Yucatán (Mexico).

Height: Up to 15 m (50 ft).

Trunk: Straight and smooth with brownish-red bark, on whose surface appear small spots of cork.

Canopy: Perennial, shaped in a narrow oval.

Leaves: Alternate, smooth, leathery, elliptical with pointed tips, 6–15 cm (2¼–6 in) long, greenish-yellow above, paler below. The leaves are aromatic, as are those of many other members of the Lauraceae family.

Flowers: The flowers appear in axillary or terminal panicles, are creamy-white in colour and measure 5–10 mm (about ¼–½ in) in diameter. Blossoms intermittently throughout the year.

Fruit: A dark blue to black rounded drupe of about 1 cm (½ in) diameter, inserted in a yellow or red cup; contains a single seed.

Comments: Cigua is a common tree in areas of brushwood all over the island. It owes its common name to the fact that its wood and leaves smell like a type of Cuban crab also known as Cigua. Cigua fruits are eaten by cattle. Its strong, yellow wood is used for rural construction.

Coco Plumoso

(Queen Palm)
Syagrus romanzoffianus (Cham.) Glassman

Synonym: *Arecastrum romanzoffianum* Cham.
Cocos romanzoffianum Cham.
Cocos plumosa Hook.

Family: Arecaceae (Palmae)

Origin: Central and southern Brazil.

Height: Up to 6 m (20 ft), occasionally taller.

Trunk: Single, stout, smooth, slightly ringed, up to 40 cm (16 in) diameter.

Canopy: A pinnate palm.

Leaves: Very long, shaped like enormous feathers, with many long, narrow leaflets arching gracefully from the central rib. The bright green petioles are 1 m (3¼ ft) long, with fibres at their base.

Flowers: Inconspicuous, creamy-white, in bunches hanging between the leaves.

Fruit: Ovate to round, with a short beak at the end, fleshy, yellow to orange when ripe, 2–3 cm (¾–1 in) diameter, containing one round seed 1–2 cm (½–¾ in) in diameter.

Comments: Coco Plumoso is a beautiful, fast-growing ornamental palm frequently used in parks, gardens and avenues in tropical countries.

Cocotero

(Mata de Coco, Coconut Palm)
Coocos nucifera L.

Family: Arecaceae (Palmae)

Origin: Probably South America or the islands of the South Pacific or Indian Ocean.

Height: Depending on the variety, 5–20 m (16–65 ft).

Trunk: Swollen at the base, inclined, irregularly ringed, with vertical cracks.

Canopy: Pinnate palm.

Leaves: Feathery; the base expanded and wrapped with coarse woven fibre; with very long segments arranged in a row on either side of the central rib; greenish-yellow in colour; 1.5–4 m (5–13 ft) long.

Flowers: Insignificant, in bunches borne between the leaves, yellow, covered a modified leaf called the 'spathe' when young.

Fruit: Covered with a fibrous husk. Inside, a hard shell contains the liquid known as coconut milk, which fills the cavity while the fruit is young, becoming a solid, white mass lining the cavity when it is ripe. The fruit is oval to round, yellow or green; 20–30 cm (8–12 in) in diameter. The coconut itself is the seed.

Comments: The coconut palm is one of the most famous trees of the tropical world, having been cultivated for thousands of years. It is known as 'The Tree of 100 Uses'. In Cuba it is present everywhere, not only beside beaches but also in inland cities and on farms, for ornamental and for commercial purposes. In Cuba the husk and the shell are often carved by craftspeople for sale to visitors. Coconut milk is often drunk direct from the shell, either by itself or mixed with rum in the drink known locally as 'saoco'. A traditional pudding, 'dulce de coco', is made from the flesh of the coconut. In the eastern city of Baracoa 'cucuruchos de coco' are made by wrapping the fibre round a mixture of coconut, honey and other local ingredients to make a delicious sweet. The oil extracted from the dried coconut mass (known as copra) is used for cooking, for lighting, and for making soaps, shampoos and creams for skin care.

Copey

(Cupey, Balsam Fig, Pitch Apple, Autograph Tree)
Clusia rosea Jacq.

Family: Clusiaceae

Origin: Tropical America and Florida (USA).

Height: Up to 20 m (65 ft).

Trunk: Straight, smooth with numerous aerial roots containing a yellow, resinous sap.

Canopy: Rounded, densely leafed.

Leaves: Opposite, obovate, leathery, thick, notched at the tips, dark green, 10–15 cm (4–6 in) long, with a prominent central vein on both sides.

Flowers: Appearing singly or in groups of two to three flowers, each one having six to nine white, rounded petals tinted pink around the yellow heart of the flower, 8–9 cm (3–3½ in) across. The flower has a waxy appearance. Blossoms intermittently all year round.

Fruit: The spherical, creamy-white seed pod 3–8 cm (1–3 in) in diameter opens as it ripens into several sections, exposing

black seeds covered by a red membrane.

Comments: Copey is a beautiful tree found in Cuban rain forests; it is also often planted in gardens and parks for its ornamental foliage. It sometimes lives as an epiphyte on other trees, or on rocks. When the surfaces of its leaves are engraved with a pencil or nail, the resulting scar remains even after the leaf has fallen; this peculiarity is the origin of the popular name 'Autograph Tree'. It is said that the Spanish conquistadors used to play cards with marked Copey leaves. Copey is a medicinal plant: the leaves, bark and resin are used to cure chest ailments, rheumatism and broken bones.

Corojo

(Corojo espinoso)
Gastrococos crispa (Kunt) H.E. Moore

WARNING: Very prickly palm (trunk and leaves).

Family: Arecaceae (Palmae)

Origin: Cuba, endemic.

Height: 5–7 m (16–23 ft).

Trunk: Spindle-shaped, grey, very prickly when young, with alternating rings of spiny and smooth bark.

Canopy: Pinnate palm.

Leaves: Pinnate, forming a crown of about 12 leaves 2–3 m (6½–10 ft) long, each with about 100 pairs of leaflets 30–50 cm (12–20 in) long, glossy green above and paler below; the stalks are also covered with black spines.

Flowers: The small yellow flowers appear in large quantities in racemes about 80 cm (32 in) long, which hang among the leaves. Blossoms in June to July.

Fruit: Rounded, yellowish-brown when ripe, 2.5–3 cm (about 1 in) in diameter; the inner layer surrounding the single seed is very hard.

Comments: This curious palm is grown widely on chalky soils all over the country, mainly in the Eastern provinces, where the excellent oil contained in the seed is extracted for cooking. The nut contained in the fruit is edible (if you can break its shell!), and a pudding called 'cocada' is made from the seeds. The fibres of the leaves are used for rope-making. A related species (*Acrocomia pilosa*), also commonly known as Corojo, is endemic to Cuba and is used for the same purposes.

Dagame

Calycophyllum candidissimum (Vahl.) DC.

Family: Rubiaceae

Origin: Cuba, southern Mexico to Venezuela.

Height: Up to 12 m (40 ft).

Trunk: Straight, slender, smooth, with reddish, peeling bark.

Canopy: Tapering towards the top, with upward-growing branches.

Leaves: Opposite, simple, elliptical, bright green above and paler below, 4–13 cm (1½–5 in) long.

Flowers: The tiny, creamy-white flowers with white bracts appear in compact inflorescences, which make the tree very attractive. Blossoms in the dry season (November to December).

Fruit: The dark brown, dry seed pod is 1 cm (about ½ in) long and contains powder-like seeds.

Comments: Although seldom used as an ornamental, Dagame is one of the most enchanting of the flowering trees of Cuba; when it is in flower its branches look as though they are covered with snow and its coppery-red bark is also attractive. Dagame wood is much prized and used to be exported extensively. Now the tree is seldom found in natural conditions. Beautiful Dagame trees may be seen in the National Botanic Garden, in the Cuban Semi-deciduous Forest area.

Encina

(Encino, Oak)
Quercus oleoides subsp. *sagraeana* (Nutt.) Borhidi

Synonym: *Quercus virginiana* Mill.
Quercus cubana A. Rich.

Family: Fagaceae

Origin: Cuba, southern USA.

Height: Up to 20 m (65 ft).

Trunk: Straight, with dark brown bark.

Canopy: Rounded, evergreen.

Leaves: Alternate, elliptical, leathery, dark green and shiny above and greyish below, concave in their lower surfaces, 3–12 cm (1–4¾ in) long.

Flowers: The plant has male and female flowers appearing on the same tree. The male flowers appear as a hanging inflorescence, whereas the female ones are solitary or grouped. Blossoms in early summer (May, June).

Fruit: The large, dry, single-seeded fruits are light brown, shiny and measure up to 2.5 cm (1 in) long. They are suspended in a cup-shaped scaly structure that covers about a quarter of the fruit.

Comments: This is the only species of oak that occurs in the Tropics. As with the other members of the *Quercus* genus, its timber is of high quality. In Cuba, this species is only found growing in the acidic soils of Pinar del Río and the Isla de la Juventud, where pine forests also grow. The bark is rich in tannins and in the past was used for tanning leather; it also has the medical property of reducing fever. The wood is used for cabinet-making and building.

Fenix Robelín

(Dwarf Date Palm)
Phoenix roebelenii O'Brien

Family: Arecaceae (Palmae)

Origin: Indochina (Laos).

Height: Up to 2 m (6½ ft).

Trunk: Slender, single or clustered, partially encased in old leaf bases.

Canopy: A pinnate palm.

Leaves: Graceful, arching, feathery and slender, 1–1.5 m (3¼–5 ft) long; the leaflets are shiny, dark green, very narrow and drooping and are replaced at the basal part of the leaf by long and slender spines.

Flowers: The sexes are separated in different plants; the inflorescence appears among the leaves, with a short stem terminating in a branching cluster. Blossoms in August to September.

Fruit: A purple drupe somewhat similar in shape and texture to an olive, measuring 10–15 mm (about ½ in) long and containing one seed.

Comments: This is one of the most commonly used palms in Cuban gardens, streets and avenues; it is also used as a houseplant. It is salt-tolerant and hardy. Although it is related to the Date Palm, the fruit only has a thin layer of non-edible flesh.

Ficus Lira

(Jagüey, Fiddle-leaf Fig)
Ficus lirata Warb. ex De Wild.

Synonym: *Ficus pandurata* Sander

Family: Moraceae

Origin: Tropical Africa.

Height: Up to 10 m (33 ft) tall.

Trunk: Straight, wide, without the aerial roots that are common in other figs; the bark is dark brown.

Canopy: Rounded, densely leafed, perennial.

Leaves: Alternate, very large (up to 30 cm [12 in] long), violin-shaped, leathery, with very prominent veins and an irregular surface, glossy green above and paler below.

Flowers: The tiny flowers appear inside a rounded light green structure somewhat resembling a tennis ball; it is known as the 'receptacle'. Blooms during the rainy season.

Fruit: This tree does not fruit in Cuba, where it is propagated by means of large cuttings.

Comments: This is a beautiful tree, with large, glossy leaves. Young plants propagated from cuttings make elegant indoor plants in well-lit rooms.

Framboyán

(Flamboyán, Flamboyant, Royal Poinciana, Poinciana, Flame Tree)
Delonix regia (Bojer ex Hook.) Raf.

Family: Caesalpiniaceae (Leguminosae)

Origin: Madagascar.

Height: Up to 20 m (65 ft), usually less in Cuba.

Trunk: Branching from 2 m (6½ ft) above the base with tabular roots up to 90 cm (36 in) in diameter; smooth, light brown bark.

Canopy: Widely extended; occasionally with weeping branches.

Leaves: Alternate, compound of numerous small leaflets 4–10 mm (about ²⁄₁₀–½ in) long, the whole leaf being 30–50 cm (12–20 in) long; light green. The leaves fall during the dry season.

Flowers: Very large and showy, in numerous large axillary and terminal clusters of seven or more red-orange flowers covering the tree; the flowers have five petals, one of which is white with red spots. Blossoms from June to August, after which the new leaves appear.

Fruit: The large, pendulous, dark brown, flat, woody seed pod opens into two parts when dry, releasing the seeds.

Comments: Framboyán is one of the most decorative ornamental trees to be found in the Tropics and from early June the city of Havana glows with Framboyán blossom. The tree is planted in the countryside beside roads as well as in parks and avenues. The seed pods are used for handcrafts. Its common name, Framboyán, is derived from the French 'flamboyant'.

Framboyán Amarillo

(Yellow Flamboyant)
Peltophorum pterocarpum (DG.) Baker ex K. Heyne

Synonym: *Peltophorum ferrugineum* Benth.

Family: Caesalpiniaceae (Leguminosae)

Origin: Tropical Asia and Australia.

Height: A tree that grows up to 24 m (just under 80 ft), usually less tall in Cuba.

Trunk: Straight, up to 80 cm (32 in) in diameter; the bark is brown and rough.

Canopy: A dense, rounded canopy; perennial.

Leaves: Alternate, compound, feathery, with many small leaflets 2–2.5 cm (¾–1 in) long and 1 cm (about ½ in) wide; bright green; the new leaves and buds are coppery-red and have a velvety appearance; the entire leaf is about 50 cm (20 in) long.

Flowers: Showy, in erect racemes of 20 to 30 flowers at the ends of the branches and twigs, bright yellow, with five petals and a brown, furry stripe where they meet at the centre of the flower, frilly edges, 2–3 cm (about 1 in) across. Lightly scented. Blossoms all year round but mainly in the rainy season.

Fruit: The flat seeds are contained within a flat, coppery-red or brown seed pod measuring about 10 by 2.5 cm (4 by 1 in).

Comments: This ornamental was introduced into the island during the early part of the twentieth century by the Agronomic Station of Santiago de Las Vegas near Havana. It is a nectar-producing tree often visited by bees.

Frijolillo

(Cucharillo, Guamá Piñón, Jurabaina)
Hebestigma cubense (Kunth) Urb.

Family: Fabaceae (Leguminosae)

Origin: Cuba, endemic.

Height: A small tree 5–12 m (16–40 ft) high.

Trunk: Smooth, light brown bark, sparsely branched.

Canopy: Narrow, sparse, deciduous.

Leaves: Alternate, compound, with seven to nine ovate to spear-shaped leaflets 5–15 cm (2–6 in) long, with sharp tips, deep green above and paler beneath. The leaflets are curved with the convex side facing upwards.

Flowers: In axillary clusters 8–15 cm (3–6 in) long; each flower has a light pink corolla of five petals measuring up to 2 cm (¾ in) long. Blossoms in early spring (March) when the tree is almost bare of leaves, although leaf growth may overlap with the end of the flowering period.

Fruit: A black, bean-like seed pod 10–18 cm (4–7 in) long and 2–3 cm (about 1 in) wide, containing black seeds.

Comments: Frijolillo is an excellent timber tree with delicate pink flowers. The wood is very hard and dark. The tree owes its common name to its bean-like seed pods ('frijol' = bean). It commonly grows in dry woodland conditions.

Gavilán

(Palo Blanco, Paradise Tree, Bitterwood)
Simaruba glauca DC. var. *glauca*

Family: Simaroubaceae

Origin: West Indies, Bahamas, Florida (USA).

Height: A maximum of 16 m (52 ft).

Trunk: Slender, with reddish-brown bark.

Canopy shape: Rounded.

Leaves: Alternate, compound with 9 to 16 opposite or alternate oval leaflets 4–10 cm (1½–4 in) long and 1.5–5 cm (½–2 in) wide; the leaflets are dark, glossy green above and light grey beneath. The leaves, which are reddish when young, arch gracefully over their full length of 20–50 cm (8–20 in).

Flowers: The small, star-shaped flowers are creamy white to yellow. They appear massed in large quantities in terminal or axillary bunches. Blossoms in April to May.

Fruit: An oval drupe 1.5–2 cm (½–¾ in) long, dark purple when ripe, single-seeded.

Comments: Gavilán is a graceful tree occurring in dry forests near the coasts. It contains resins and oils. The fruit is edible but tastes rather insipid. The bark is renowned as having medicinal properties useful in the treatment of dysentery, fevers, constipation and other conditions.

Guana

Hildegardia cubensis (Urb.) Kosterm.

Synonym: *Sterculia cubensis* Urb.

Family: Malvaceae (formerly Sterculiaceae)

Origin: Cuba, endemic.

Height: Up to 15 m (50ft).

Trunk: Wide in the middle, smooth, green; up to 80 cm (32 in) maximum width.

Canopy: Oval.

Leaves: Heart-shaped, light green, about 20 cm (8 in) long. The leaves fall from the tree during the dry season.

Flowers: The small yellow flowers appear during the dry season.

Fruit: The light brown winged fruit, which measures 2–4 cm (¾–1½ in) long, is dispersed by the wind.

Comments: This beautiful Cuban tree grows in Las Tunas and Holguín provinces. In the former the Guana is rare, due to the extensive use of its bark for the manufacture of shoes, ropes, etc. by both local people and the freedom fighters – 'Mambises' – who fought in Cuba's nineteenth century wars of independence. Nowadays, the Guana is a protected tree. It can be seen in the forests along the northern coast of Holguín.

Guano de Costa

(Miraguano de Lana, Thatch Palm, Peaberry Palm)
Thrinax radiata Lodd. ex Schult. & Schult. f.

Synonym: *Thrinax parviflora* Sw.

Family: Arecaceae (Palmae)

Origin: Cuba, Hispaniola, Jamaica, Bahamas, southern Florida (USA) and Yucatán (Mexico).

Height: Up to 5 m (16 ft), occasionally taller.

Trunk: Single, slender, smooth, grey, up to 15 cm (6 in) in diameter, rising from an accumulated mass of old roots at its base.

Canopy: Palmate palm.

Leaves: Large, round, fan-shaped leaves 1 m (3¼ ft) in diameter on long, slender stalks. The upper surfaces are bright green, while the undersides of the leaves are a paler shade.

Flowers: Extremely small, creamy white, on branched stalks that are longer than the leaves.

Fruit: The round, white, fleshy fruits about 7 mm (³/₁₀ in) in diameter are attached to branches of the flower stalk. The seeds are round and smooth, with a central cavity inside.

Comments: A graceful palm, which grows beside Cuba's sandy beaches and on the cays off the coast. The Guanahacabibes Peninsula is a particularly beautiful coastal landscape where the Guano de Costa grows profusely. The palms' leaves are extremely durable and are used for making hats, while their stalks are used for the construction of houses and fences. The word *Thrinax* is Greek for fan.

Guao

(Guao de Sabana, Guao Prieto, Guao Hediondo)
Comocladia dentata Jacq.

WARNING: This plant has highly toxic sap.

Family: Anacardiaceae

Origin: Cuba and Hispaniola.

Height: Up to 12 m (40 ft).

Trunk: Straight, slender, with dark brown furrowed bark; sometimes grows as a shrub.

Canopy: The leaves are grouped at the ends of branches.

Leaves: Alternate, compound of seven to eight pairs of brilliant, leathery leaflets with serrated edges, 3–10 cm (1–4 in) long. The veins are very prominent on the upper surface; the lower surface is slightly furry.

Flowers: Appear in terminal reddish panicles 20–25 cm (8–10 in) long; the

flowers are stemless, grouped in clusters and quite inconspicuous. Blossoms all year round, mostly during the rainy season.

Fruit: A rounded drupe 7–8 cm (about 3 in) long.

Comments: Guao is an Indian word for the family of plants known as Anacardiaceae; all of them have highly poisonous, caustic sap that burns the skin. Some people are so allergic to Guao that even standing near it harms them. Nevertheless, the fruits are eaten by animals and the wood is very hard and resistant. Guao occurs all over the island on the coast, in savannas and in woods, so watch out!

Guásima

(Bastard Cedar)
Guazuma ulmifolia Lam.

Synonym: *Guazuma tomentosa* Kunth

Family: Malvaceae (formerly Sterculiaceae)

Origin: Tropical and subtropical continental and insular America.

Height: Up to 20 m (65 ft).

Trunk: Profusely branched from 1 to 2 m (about 3–6 ft) above the foot of the tree; up to 60 cm (24 in) in diameter, rough bark.

Canopy: Open, spreading branches.

Leaves: Oval, asymmetric at their base with serrated edges and tapering points, occasionally hairy, light green, 3–15 cm (1–6 in) long.

Flowers: Tiny, appearing in bunches at the axils of the leaves, yellow and fragrant.

Fruit: Black, woody, spherical, with a rough surface, measuring 2–3 cm (¾–1 in) across.

Comments: Guásima is a very common tree along roadsides, in pastures and in woods. In the past, its timber was used in the countryside for many different purposes. Its sticky juice was used to cure dysentery; it is also useful for treating burns.

Guasimilla

(Majagüilla Macho)
Trichospermum mexicanum Baill.

Synonym: *Belotia greviaefolia* A. Rich.

Family: Tiliaceae

Origin: Western Cuba, endemic.

Height: Up to 15 m (50 ft).

Trunk: Branching at 2 m (6½ ft) or less from the base, grey, smooth, about 30 cm (12 in) in diameter; the twigs that grow from the branches have a furry surface.

Canopy: Dense, in the shape of an umbrella.

Leaves: Perennial, with a short petiole, alternate, elliptic, rounded at the base with three veins arising from the base and with sharp tips; the leaves are 8–12 cm (about 3–5 in) long and 3–6 cm (1–2¼ in) wide, the margins are serrated. The leaves are light green on their upper surface, and furry and paler beneath.

Flowers: Small, less than 2 cm (¾ in) long, grouped in small bunches of about 2–10 cm (¾–4 in) growing in the axils of the leaves at the terminal parts of the

twigs. The flowers are pale pink–mauve, with five free sepals and petals. Blossoms in November to January, sometimes before.

Fruit: A small (2–3 cm wide, 1.5–2 cm long [about 1 in by ¾ in]) brown capsule somewhat heart-shaped ending in a pointed tip and furry at the surface. When dry, it opens into two valves. The seeds are black, surrounded by straight, short golden hairs, and look like minuscule spiders.

Comments: Guasimilla is a very handsome tree that deserves much more attention by garden designers. It is fast growing and, when in full bloom, offers a beautiful combination of pale green leaves and pale pink–mauve flowers. In the wild, it grows in the semi-deciduous forests of Western Cuba, on acidic soils.

Guayaba

(Guayabo, Guava)
Psidium guajava L.

Family: Myrtaceae

Origin: Tropical America.

Height: Up to 5–6 m (16–20 ft).

Trunk: Slender, short, profusely branched, with a smooth light brown bark.

Canopy: Rounded and leafy.

Leaves: Opposite, elliptical, the tips may be sharp or blunt; the leaves are dull green on the upper surface, with prominent veins, and measure 7–14 cm (2¾–5½ in) long.

Flowers: Appearing singly or doubly in the leaf axils. The flowers have four to five white petals 1.5–2 cm (½–¾ in) wide, with numerous white and yellow stamens appearing at their centre; they look rather like brushes. Flowers sporadically throughout the year, usually during the wetter months.

Fruit: A large, rounded fruit 3–6 cm (1–2¼ in) in diameter, which turns from green to yellow when ripe; the edible flesh is pink or pale yellow, and contains numerous small, hard seeds around its centre.

Comments: Guayaba is the commonest fruit tree in Cuba, having been naturalized in pre-Columbian times when the Indians brought it to the island from the South American continent. It is found occurring naturally in fields and woods, and is also cultivated in domestic gardens and on large fruit farms. Guayaba fruit, which is very rich in Vitamin C, can be eaten raw and in drinks or cooked in jellies and desserts. The wood is compact and resistant and is used in the countryside for building and cabinet-making. The bark and leaves contain tannins, and are used by practitioners of traditional medicine to heal wounds and to cure diarrhoea and stomach pain. A related native species, the fruit of which is highly aromatic, is renowned for its use in the preparation of 'Guayabita del Pinar', a rum-based liquor. During the manufacture of the drink, small fruits are inserted into the bottles.

Güira

(Totuma, Calabash Tree)
Crescentia cujete L.

Family: Bignoniaceae

Origin: Tropical America and Florida (USA).

Height: Up to 10 m (33 ft), usually less.

Trunk: Smooth, light brown, with branches extending from it at random intervals.

Canopy: Extended, with spreading branches.

Leaves: Clusters of three to five leaves appear in whorls along the stems; they are spatula or spoon shaped, measure up to 15 cm (6 in) long and are dark green in colour.

Flowers: Growing directly from the trunk and branches, the flowers open at night and fall off in the early morning. They are pale violet or yellow, bell-shaped with five lobes, 5–6 cm (just over 2 in) in diameter

and pollinated by bats. Güira blooms all year round.

Fruit: Varying widely in size, the rounded seed pods have a hard outer shell and are filled with a pulp containing numerous seeds.

Comments: Güira is a very popular tree. The shells of the fruits, known as 'Jícaras', are used by country-dwellers for many purposes: as vessels for salt and sugar, as cups for coffee and as 'maracas' (percussion instruments). Güira pulp mixed with honey is used as a medicinal remedy for chest infections.

Jagua

(Marmalade Box)
Genipa americana L.

Family: Rubiaceae

Origin: Tropical America.

Height: 6–14 m (20–46 ft).

Trunk: Straight, with numerous stout branches; the bark is brown.

Canopy: Rounded, leafy, deciduous.

Leaves: Opposite, leathery, spear-shaped, 10–35 cm (4–14 in) long and 5–19 cm (2–7½ in) wide, deep, dull green above and paler below, with sharp tips.

Flowers: The white flowers appear in short inflorescences; each flower has a bell-shaped calyx with five lobes. The blooms are strongly scented and appear from April to June.

Fruit: A large, elliptical berry measuring 6–7 cm (about 2½ in) long, the skin is yellowish-brown with rather a slimy

appearance; the sour pulp contains numerous seeds.

Comments: Jagua is grown as a fruit tree: jam, juice and liqueur are produced from the ripe berries, which also have medicinal properties. The copper-coloured timber is very hard and many agricultural tools are made from it. The original Indian inhabitants of Cuba used the juice of the young fruit to dye textiles and for tattoos. Jagua is an Indian word that also appears throughout the island as a place name; an example of this is the Castillo de Jagua in Cienfuegos.

Jagüey Hembra

(Strangler Fig, Golden Fig, Wild Fig)
Ficus aurea Nutt.

WARNING: The milky sap in the leaves, trunk and branches can cause irritation to the eyes and skin.

Family: Moraceae

Origin: West Indies, Bahamas and Florida (USA).

Height: Up to 20 m (65 ft) tall.

Trunk: Grey to light brown with smooth bark and milky sap.

Canopy: Perennial, rounded, broad and leafy.

Leaves: Alternate, elliptical, dark, glossy greenish-yellow, with yellow veins, 5–15 cm (2–6 in) long and 2.5–8 cm (1–3 in) wide.

Flowers: Very small, enclosed in a spherical structure known as the 'receptacle' located at the leaf axils, about 5–10 mm (¼–½ in) in diameter, having a hole at the upper end through which the pollinating insect enters to fertilize the female flowers during the rainy season.

Fruit: A spherical, berry-like fruit of about 1 cm (½ in) in diameter known as a 'sycone'; bright yellow or red, containing small brown seeds.

Comments: In Cuba there are about 12 native species of figs, which grow profusely in rain forests and alongside rivers and creeks. The 'Jagüeyes' are mainly epiphytic plants. When a seed sprouts on a tree it sends down aerial roots to the ground that join together to form a trunk, finally killing the host tree; it is for this reason that they are known as 'Strangler Figs'.

Jata de Guanabacoa

(Palma Jata, Cuban Petticoat Palm)
Copernicia macroglossa H. Wendl.

Synonym: *Copernicia torreana* León

Family: Arecaceae (Palmae)

Origin: Cuba, endemic.

Height: About 8 m (26 ft).

Trunk: Covered by a thick mat of dead leaves, which hang down around the trunk.

Canopy: A twisted spiral mass of palmate leaves.

Leaves: Numerous, extremely large (up to 2 m [6½ ft]), bright green, without stalks, closely packed together, with minute spines along the edges of each segment.

Flowers: Inconspicuous, sunken in the hairy surface of large arching inflorescences. Blossoms May to June.

Fruit: A golden-yellow rounded drupe of about 2.5 cm (1 in) diameter, containing a single seed.

Comments: This spectacular palm is endemic to Central Cuba in wooded areas near rivers. It may be cultivated and has a dramatic appearance, but its slow growth is a handicap to its use as an ornamental plant.

Jocuma

(Caguaní, Mastic, Jungle Plum, Wild Olive)
Sideroxylon foetidissimum Jacq.

Synonym: *Mastichodendron foetidissimum* (Jacq.) Cronq.

Family: Sapotaceae

Origin: West Indies and Florida (USA).

Height: Up to 25 m (80 ft), commonly less.

Trunk: Straight, with scaly reddish bark.

Canopy: Rounded and leafy, perennial.

Leaves: Alternate, oval, with undulating edges and pale yellow veins; glossy, yellowish-green, 5–15 cm (2–6 in) long. The leaves are clustered around the ends of the branches and twigs.

Flowers: Small and inconspicuous, grouped in the axils of the leaves. The corolla is pale yellowish-green and less

than 1 cm (4/10 in) wide. Blossoms mainly in the dry season.

Fruit: The rounded to oval berry about 2–2.5 cm (¾–1 in) long contains a white, juicy, sticky edible flesh, in which is embedded a single round, brown seed.

Comments: Jocuma is a tall, native hardwood tree that grows in wooded lowland areas. Its orange-coloured timber is hard and heavy and is widely used for construction. The species' scientific name *foetidissimum* refers to the disagreeable odour of the flowers, leaves and bark.

Jubabán

(Cabo de Hacha, Wild Mahogany)
Trichilia hirta L.

Family: Meliaceae

Origin: Tropical America.

Height: Small tree of about 10 m (33 ft) height.

Trunk: Straight, with rough, brown, furrowed bark; up to 40 cm (16 in) in diameter.

Canopy: Round, with dense foliage.

Leaves: Compound, with numerous leaflets with sharp tips, asymmetrical at their base, arranged in spirals; vivid green above, paler green below; about 30 cm (12 in) long.

Flowers: Pale greenish-white, inconspicuous; fragrant, rich in nectar. The tree flowers during the rainy season and is very attractive to insects.

Fruit: Round greenish-brown seed pods with three cavities hairy at the interior, containing one seed each: 10–13 mm (about ½ in) in diameter. The black seeds are covered with a brilliant, red, fleshy mass (the aril).

Comments: The Jubabán grows throughout the Cuban archipelago, in forests both in the mountains and in flatter areas of the island. Its seeds are dispersed by birds attracted by the fleshy red cover of the seed. The Jubabán has clear brown-reddish heartwood surrounded by white wood; it is used for making toys, kitchen tools and axe handles. The related species *Trichilia havanensis*, known as 'Siguaraya', flourishes in the same ecosystems, but flowers in the dry season, which effectively prevents the two species being crossed.

Júcaro

Bucida subinermis Bisse

Family: Combretaceae

Origin: Endemic to Cuba.

Height: About 12 m (40 ft).

Trunk: Straight, short, with numerous branches and very scaly brown bark.

Canopy: Wide with ascending branches, densely leafed. Deciduous for a very short time in the dry season.

Leaves: Alternate, grouped in whorls at the ends of twigs, armed with two to three short spines; the leaves are 2–4 cm (¾–1½ in) long, spatulate with a rounded or notched tip, bright green above and dull green below.

Flowers: Very tiny and inconspicuous in axillary or terminal spikes.

Fruit: A small nut 3–4 mm (less than ²⁄₁₀ in) long.

Comments: Júcaro is one of the finest timber trees in Cuba. It is also planted for shade in parks and gardens in spite of the great quantity of dead leaves and flower spikes that the tree produces. Júcaro is found in the wild on the damp plains and woods of the Eastern and Central provinces.

Laurel de la India

(Laurel, Benjamina, Jagüey, Weeping Fig)
Ficus benjamina L.

Family: Moraceae

Origin: India and Malaysia.

Height: Up to 30 m (100 ft), usually less in Cuba.

Trunk: Massive, wide, with pendant aerial roots; the bark is light brown.

Canopy: The densely leafed branches arch gracefully in a 'weeping' form.

Leaves: Alternate; deep, glossy green in colour, elliptical with pointed tips, 5–8 cm (2–3 in) long.

Flowers: As in other figs, the flowers are contained in the 'receptacles', which measure less than 1 cm (about ½ in) in diameter. They are rounded, reddish-purple, and appear all year round.

Fruit: In Cuba the fruits do not appear because of the lack of a pollinator insect. The tree is easily propagated asexually.

Comments: This tree is ubiquitous throughout all Cuban cities and beside old country roads. The roots are invasive and cause considerable damage to underground piping and to pavements. This tree is easily shaped by pruning into topiary forms, as may be seen in the Avenida de los Presidentes and Quinta Avenida in the city of Havana.

Lirio

(Lirio de Costa, Frangipán, Súcheli, Lirio Tricolor, Frangipani, Pagoda Tree, Temple Tree)
Plumeria rubra L.

WARNING: Do not get the milky sap in your eyes.

Family: Apocynaceae

Origin: Central and South America.

Height: A small tree up to 3 m (10 ft) tall.

Trunk: Branching profusely from 1 m (3¼ ft) of growth, slender, with smooth light brown bark; contains milky sap.

Canopy: Rounded and open.

Leaves: Grouped at the ends of the branches, obovate, with sharp tips and narrowed bases. The upper side is brilliant green with yellowish central and lateral veins and a prominent marginal vein; the lower side is paler with a very prominent central vein; the total length is 12–50 cm (5–20 in), and the width up to 15 cm (6 in).

Flowers: Highly decorative, in large terminal clusters of ten flowers or more, each one having five petals about 4 cm (1½ in) long, commonly with shading to yellow at their centres. The colours of the flowers include white, yellow, pink, rose-red, pinkish-yellow and purple; the flowers are strongly scented. Blossoms from May to August.

Fruit: The seed pods, formed of two long, cylindrical halves with sharp tips united at their bases and measuring 9–30 cm (3½–12 in) long, are full of small winged seeds. Lirio may also be propagated from large cuttings.

Comments: This is one of the most widely cultivated small ornamental trees in the Tropics. In some Asiatic countries it is used in cemeteries, but this is not the case in Cuba, where it is often planted near the sea.

Magnolia

(Large-flowered Magnolia)
Magnolia grandiflora L.

Family: Magnoliaceae

Origin: Southern North America.

Height: A tree that can grow to 25 m (80 ft) in its natural habitat; in Cuba it reaches 3–5 m (10–16 ft) or even less.

Trunk: Short branches grow from the first few metres of the trunk; the bark is brown and spotted with lichens.

Canopy: Perennial, a rounded to narrow canopy.

Leaves: The leaves are alternate, large, elliptical to ovate with sharp tips. They are thick and glossy, being deep, brilliant green above and brown below, and measure 10–20 cm (4–8 in) long and 7–10 cm (2¾–4 in) wide. Magnolia is an evergreen tree.

Flowers: The large single flowers have numerous ivory-coloured petals arranged in a spiral; they are slightly concave with rounded tips. The flower, which appears in late summer, is strongly scented and grows to up to 25 cm (10 in) wide.

Fruit: The woody cone-like fruit has brilliant red seeds suspended in cavities spirally disposed within the structure of the cone.

Comments: This magnificent tree is renowned for its large and fragrant flowers. *Magnolia* is one of the most primitive living angiosperm genera of trees; the genus has undergone little evolutionary change for 100 million years, since the time when dinosaurs walked the Earth.

Majagua

(Majagua Azul, Blue Mahoe, Cuba Bark, Mountain Mahoe)
Talipariti elatum (Sw.) Fryxell

Synonym: *Hibiscus elatus* Sw.

Family: Malvaceae

Origin: Cuba and Jamaica.

Height: A tall tree that grows up to about 25 m (80 ft).

Trunk: Straight, stout, branched, with furrowed brown bark.

Canopy: Perennial; with a rounded canopy.

Leaves: Alternate, heart-shaped, bright green above and greyish beneath, with clearly marked veins. The leaves grow to 8–20 cm (3–8 cm) long and to roughly the same width.

Flowers: Showy, the calyx having five lobes 3–5 cm (1–2 in) long and the large, five-petalled corolla measuring 8–12 cm (3–5 in). The stamens are fused into a column, only parting towards the outer

end. The flowers are orange-yellow or orange-red, fading to deep crimson before they fall from the tree. Blooms in the dry season.

Fruit: A dry, hairy, spherical seed pod divided into five parts, which contains several furry seeds.

Comments: Majagua is a common tree in Cuban rain forests and is cultivated for its high-quality timber. It is sometimes used as an ornamental for its numerous beautiful flowers and perennial foliage. Its bluish-green wood is used for building and making furniture. The flowers, roots and bark have numerous medicinal purposes.

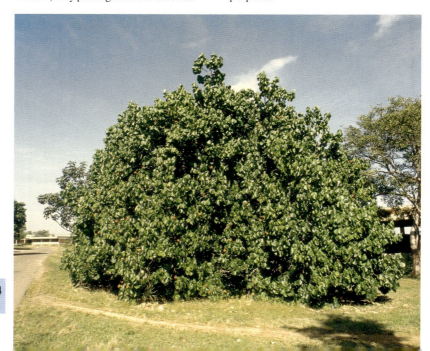

Mamey Colorado

(Sapote, Mamey, Zapote)
Pouteria sapota (Jacq.) H.E. Moore & Stearn

Family: Sapotaceae

Origin: Central America.

Height: Up to 30 m (100 ft) tall, less in Cuba.

Trunk: Straight, thick, branching, with deeply furrowed brown bark.

Canopy: Rounded, deciduous, densely leafed, with milky sap in the young parts.

Leaves: Alternate, tightly grouped at the ends of the branches, in twigs with the new growth being hairy and having a reddish tinge. The leaves are large, obovate to elliptical with sharp tips, deep green with prominent veins, and 15–25 cm (6–10 in) long.

Flowers: Inconspicuous, creamy white, stemless, densely grouped on the twigs. Flowers in September to October.

Fruit: A large berry in the shape of a rugby ball, with a coarse, brown, sandy-textured skin. The large, lustrous dark brown seed is surrounded by soft, sweet, red flesh that tastes deliciously of dates. The whole fruit is 15–20 cm (6–8 in) long. It takes almost a year to ripen, after the fall of the leaves.

Comment: Mamey Colorado is one of Cuba's most popular fruits. It is eaten raw, in drinks and in ice creams. Several popular Cuban songs refer to its delectably sweet taste. The seed contains a medicinal oil used in hair treatments; the timber is dense and reddish in colour and is used for rural carpentry.

Mango

Mangifera indica L.

Family: Anacardiaceae

Origin: Tropical Asia (Malaysia and India).

Height: Varies according to the variety.

Trunk: Short, stout, with branches growing from the first metre of growth; the bark is brown, rough and scaly. The tree is resinous.

Canopy: Rounded, densely leafed; the new leaves are bright red and shiny.

Leaves: Alternate, elliptical or spear-shaped according to variety, leathery, with sharp tips, glossy green, 12–20 cm (5–8 in) long.

Flowers: The attractive inflorescences appear at the ends of the twigs in panicles of small light-green to creamy-white flowers. They are often visited by bees for their abundant nectar. Blossoms from December to February.

Fruit: Vary in shape and size according to their variety. The fruit of the mango is a large drupe with lustrous yellow skin and a thick layer of yellow pulp surrounding the central seed; it is highly aromatic and delicious to eat. The fruits ripen during the rainy season.

Comments: The Mango was introduced into Cuba at the beginning of the eighteenth century. It is the commonest fruit on the island, grows spontaneously all over the country and is known as the 'Apple of the Tropics'. Mango fruit may be eaten straight from the tree or made into chutneys, juice, sweets and puddings. The leaves and resin have medicinal properties; the trees are also planted for shade.

Miraguano

(Yuraguana)
Coccothrinax miraguama (Kunth) Becc.

Family: Arecaceae (Palmae)

Origin: Cuba and Hispaniola.

Height: Up to 5 m (16 ft).

Trunk: Single, slender, straight and smooth when adult, covered by the coarse woven fibres of the leaf sheaths.

Canopy: A palmate palm.

Leaves: Large, circular, rigid, with a long, thin petiole; the segments are narrow, divided and pointed at the tips, dull green above and silvery grey below. The entire leaf may grow to 1 m (3¼ ft) long.

Flowers: The tiny, creamy-white flowers appear in drooping racemes about 30 cm (12 in) long among the leaves. Blossoms April to June.

Fruit: Rounded pink to dark purple drupes about 1 cm (½ in) in diameter containing a single, wrinkled white seed about 8 mm (3/10 in) in diameter.

Comments: The Miraguano is a common palm in Cuba, widespread in arid and well-drained soils in coastal and riverside woods, savannas and pine forests. Miraguano is a graceful palm extremely suitable for landscape gardening, but it is not widely popular due to its slow rate of growth. The leaf of the Miraguano is used in the countryside to make brushes and brooms and for weaving hats, and the trunk is used for building. Cuba is the principal evolutionary centre of the genus *Coccothrinax*, possessing over 30 endemic species.

Nogal de la India

(Nogal Negro, Nuez, Varnish Tree, Candlenut, Walnut)
Aleurites triloba Forst.

Synonym: *Aleurites moluccana* (L.) Willd.

Family: Euphorbiaceae

Origin: India.

Height: Up to 20 m (65 ft), usually less in Cuba.

Trunk: Straight, with brownish-grey bark bearing longitudinal fissures.

Canopy: Rounded, with dense foliage.

Leaves: Glossy yellowish-green to silver, growing alternately from the twigs, with a similar shape to those of the maple. The leaves of Nogal de la India have long petioles and an extended central lobe; the whole leaf measures 5–25 cm (2–10 in).

Flowers: Small, white and numerous, arranged in branching, slightly furry racemes of an equal length to the petioles of the leaves, with five petals and numerous stamens. Blossoms April to June.

Fruit: A fleshy triangular fruit 3–4 cm (1– 1½ in) wide, with one or two very oily, hard-shelled seeds resembling walnuts.

Comments: This tree is very common in Cuba where its attractive, dense foliage makes it useful for ornamentation and for the provision of shade. The seeds contain large quantities of oil with purgative properties, which in the past were also used for the production of varnish. When lit with a match the seed burns steadily like a candle, hence the name 'Candlenut'. This is the national tree of Hawaii.

Ocuje

Calophyllum antillanum Britton

Synonym: *Calophyllum brasiliense* Camb. var. *antillanum* (Britton) Standl.

Family: Clusiaceae

Origin: West Indies.

Height: Up to 20 m (65 ft).

Trunk: Straight, stout, with dark brown furrowed bark.

Canopy: Narrow to rounded, densely leafy.

Leaves: Opposite, elliptical with rounded tips, shiny green, 5–8 cm (2–3 in) long and 3–5 cm (1–2 in) wide.

Flowers: Tiny, appearing in axillary inflorescences 4–5 cm (1½–2 in) long bearing 7 to 15 fragrant white flowers with numerous yellow stamens. Blossoms in the summer (June to August).

Fruit: A rounded drupe 2 cm (¾ in) in diameter, green to yellow when ripe.

Comments: The Ocuje is found all over Cuba, in rain forests, beside rivers, and in parks and along pavements in cities. The tree is also planted for reforestation purposes and the timber is very valuable; it is of a reddish hue, solid, resistant and often used in general carpentry. The fruits of the Ocuje are frequently fed to pigs and its resin is used to heal wounds.

Orquídea Silvestre

(Bauhinia, Casco de Buey, Butterfly Tree, Orchid Tree, Ox or Bull Hoof Tree)
Bauhinia spp.

Family: Caesalpiniaceae (Leguminosae)

Origin: India, Southeast Asia.

Height: Up to 8 m (26 ft).

Trunk: Short, slender, with numerous branches.

Canopy: Rounded and neat.

Leaves: Alternate, large, broad, divided into two lobes (shaped like a bull's hoof), pale dull green, leathery, of differing sizes.

Flowers: Extremely attractive, appearing in racemes, mainly at the ends of the branches. The blooms have a form similar to that of an orchid, having five purple, pink, lavender, yellow or white petals spotted with purple, red or yellow and exposed stamens and pistils.

Fruit: Long, bean-like, flat seed pods ending in a beak, containing round, flat seeds.

Comments: These plants are cultivated throughout the island. The two most common species are *Bauhinia variegata* and *B. purpurea*. The generic name *Bauhinia* was dedicated by Karl von Linné (the Father of Botanical Nomenclature) to the Swiss brothers Jean and Casper Bauhin, whose respective merits in botany were as identical as the two lobes of the leaf of these plants.

Palma Areca

(Areca Palm, Golden Cane Palm)
Dypsis lutescens (H.Wendl.) Beentje & J. Dransf.

Synonym: *Chrysalidocarpus lutescens* H. Wendl.

Family: Arecaceae (Palmae)

Origin: Madagascar.

Height: 5–10 m (16–33 ft).

Trunk: Grow in clumps similar to those of the bamboo, yellow to pale green, waxy. Noticeably ringed. 8–15 cm (3–6 in) diameter.

Canopy: Pinnate palm.

Leaves: Feather-like, arching, greenish-yellow with a single row of leaflets on each side of the leaf axis; crownshaft pale green to yellow, waxy; complete leaf 1–2 m (about 3–6 ft) long.

Flowers: Tiny creamy-yellow flowers in extensively branched yellow-orange bunches rising among the leaves; the tree blossoms in July and August.

Fruit: Deep yellow to orange when ripe, egg-shaped, 1.5–2 cm (½–¾ in) long; single-seeded, sweet to the taste when very ripe in August–September.

Comments: This ornamental palm is commonly cultivated in gardens all over Cuba. The young palms are used as indoor plants in houses and public buildings, and form the nucleus of a flourishing commercial plant nursery activity. Another species of the same genus often cultivated in Cuba is *Dypsis lucubensis*. Popularly known as 'Palma de Anillo' (Ring Palm), its stout single trunk bears numerous rings. It has pale green waxy leaves with curled leaflets which appear in groups of three, and black fruit.

Palma Barrigona

(Barrigona, Barrigona de Vueltabajo)
Colpothrinax wrightii Gris. & Wendl.

Family: Arecaceae (Palmae)

Origin: Cuba, endemic.

Height: Up to 15 m (50 ft) when very old.

Trunk: The bark, which is brown, rough and furrowed on the young tree, falls off as it matures, being replaced by a grey, smooth surface. The lower half of the trunk is slender, it swells at the centre, then tapers again towards the top.

Canopy: Palmate palm.

Leaves: The fan-like leaves have long stalks that are sheathed in reddish-brown fibre woven like fabric at their base; the leaf is composed of 50 segments divided to about a third of their length. They are dull green, about 1 m (3 ft) long, with ragged tips.

Flowers: Growing inconspicuously among the leaves, creamy-white, appearing in hanging racemes that are initially green but turn first yellow then orange as they mature. Blossoms in the rainy season.

Fruit: Rounded, black when ripe, about 2 cm (¾ in) in diameter.

Comments: This interesting palm grows in savannas and pine forests on sandy soils in Pinar del Río and the Isla de la Juventud. It is useful to country-dwellers for a number of reasons: the leaves are used for thatching, the wide part of the trunk is used as posts for houses, for grinding coffee and rice and for holding water, and the fruits are fed to the pigs.

Palma Cana

(Guano Cana, Cabbage Palm, Palmetto Palm)
Sabal palmetto (Walt.) Lodd.

Family: Arecaceae (Palmae)

Origin: Cuba, Bahamas and southeast USA.

Height: Up to 20 m (65 ft) or more.

Trunk: Cylindrical, smooth, thick, greyish with spots of lichen, the upper part festooned with the stalks of fallen leaves.

Canopy: Rounded, dense, formed by costapalmate leaves.

Leaves: The large arching leaves grow up to 2 m (6½ ft) long and are edged with thin, white cords known as 'canas'. The petioles are usually costapalmate: long, split at their bases and protruding deep into the dull green leaf blade. The segments are long, pointed and split at their tips.

Flowers: Inconspicuous, on long, branching racemes growing among the leaves, as long as the leaves or even longer. Blooms June to July.

Fruit: The dry, spherical, brown fruits, 8 mm (3/10 in) in diameter, contain shiny dark brown seeds.

Comments: Palma Cana is a very common palm in Cuba, growing profusely in flat areas, and is used by country-dwellers for thatching their houses. A closely related species, *Sabal maritima*, also commonly known as Palma Cana, partly shares the distribution area of *S. palmetto* and is used for the same purposes.

Palma de Abanico

(Livistona, Chinese Fan Palm)
Livistona chinensis (Jacq.) R. Br., ex Mart.

Family: Palmae (Arecaceae)

Origin: South China.

Height: Up to 5–10 m (16–33 ft).

Trunk: Single, stout, rough, irregularly ringed, often inclined, swollen at the base, about 40 cm (16 in) in diameter.

Canopy: Palmate palm.

Leaves: Like enormous fans of about 1.5 m (5 ft) in diameter, with the tip of each segment of the 'fan' drooping gracefully. The petioles are usually armed with spines and are wrapped with fibre at their bases. Once the leaves have withered they remain hanging from the trunk for some time.

Flowers: Inconspicuous, appearing in bunches among the leaves, with long stalks.

Fruit: Almost round, fleshy, 3 cm (1 in) long, dark blue-green when ripe, almost black if very ripe. Each fruit contains one round seed.

Comments: This ornamental palm is widely cultivated in Cuba. The broad, shiny leaves with drooping tips, together with its easy germination and swift growth, make it very popular with gardeners. Young Fan Palms are also used as houseplants.

Palma de Alcanfor

(Palma Sagú, Sago Palm)
Cycas revoluta Thumb.

WARNING: The seeds are poisonous.

Family: Cycadaceae

Origin: Asia, South Pacific.

Height: Up to 3 m (10 ft), usually less.

Trunk: Stout, straight, sparsely branched, marked with scars where leaves have been attached to the bark.

Canopy: Palmate.

Leaves: Forming a beautiful terminal crown at the summit of the trunk, like a palm tree, the leaves are 1–3 m (about 3–10 ft) long, and 40–50 cm (16–20 in) wide, made up of 80 to 120 deep green linear leaflets. The leaves can remain on the tree for up to three years.

Flowers: This primitive plant does not have true flowers, and the reproductive structures are found in separate plants. The male plant has a large cone (about 80 cm [32 in] long) composed of numerous scale-like structures spirally disposed; these contain the pollen sacs. The female plant has a crown of spreading, light brown modified leaves, which bear the ovules along their edges.

Fruit: Palma de Alcanfor does not bear true fruit; the naked seeds are formed along the edges of the modified leaves of the female plant.

Comments: The tree grows very slowly but it can live for hundreds of years. The trunk contains a starchy substance and a sticky resin. The rhizome also contains starch. Leaves of the Palma de Alcanfor are used in Catholic festivals and also for funeral decorations. Another common species is *Cycas circinalis*, which is also often cultivated under the name Palma de Alcanfor.

Palma de Corcho

(Corcho)
Microcycas calocoma (Miq.) A. DC.

Family: Zamiaceae

Origin: Cuba, endemic.

Height: 1–6 m (3¼–20 ft), rarely taller.

Trunk: Single, sometimes branching once or twice, the bark is smooth and greyish at the basal (older) part of the trunk, and increasingly covered by the remains of dead leaves as it progresses upwards.

Canopy: A crown of numerous (10 to 50) leaves; deciduous every two or three years.

Leaves: Long, feathery leaves 60–100 cm (24–40 in) long with petioles measuring about 10 cm (4 in), and numerous narrow, spear-shaped leaflets 8–20 cm (3–8 in) long and 5–8 mm (about ¼ in) wide, furry when young, brilliant green above and paler beneath. The leaf axis remains on the tree for four to five years after the leaflets have fallen.

Flowers: In this plant, as in all gymnosperms, real flowers do not exist. The male and female reproductive structures are called 'strobyls' and appear in different plants; both are cone-shaped and take considerable time to develop.

Fruit: Real fruits are absent, as in all gymnosperms. The female cone-like strobyl bears the pink, waxy seeds 2–3 cm (¾–1 in) long and 1–1.8 cm (½–¾ in) wide.

Comments: Palma de Corcho is only found among the vegetation growing on the 'mogotes', outcrops of limestone to be seen in the province of Pinar del Rio. The tree has been declared a Natural Monument. Its name, 'Cork Palm', refers to the abundant cork with which its trunk is surrounded. This tree is included in CITES Appendix 1 and 2 and its collection is thus strictly regulated. The National Botanical Garden makes great efforts to conserve this natural jewel, which has been declared 'at critical risk of extinction' by the World Conservation Union (IUCN).

Palma de Santa Lucía

(Palma de Guinea, Guano de Guinea, Buccaneer Palm, Hog Palm, Sargent Cherry Palm)
Pseudophoenix sargentii H. Wendl. ex Sargent

Family: Arecaceae (Palmae)

Origin: Cuba, Bahamas, Florida Cays (USA), West Indies and Yucatán (Mexico).

Height: Up to 5 m (16 ft), but usually much less.

Trunk: Spindle-like, smooth, bluish to greyish-green, prominently ringed, slightly bulging.

Canopy: A pinnate palm.

Leaves: Very large, arching, 1.5 m (5 ft) long, with rigid stems. The dull bluish-green leaflets appear in groups of two or three.

Flowers: Small, yellow-green, arranged between the leaves in wide, branching racemes on stalks 1–1.5 m (3¼–5 ft) long. Blossoms August to September.

Fruit: Rounded, orange to red, spherical or lobed in divisions of two to three, about 1.5 cm (½ in) in diameter.

Comments: This attractive little palm grows on Cuba's northern coasts and cays from Ciego de Avila to Guantánamo. Its growth is very slow and it is thus seldom used as an ornamental plant, despite its beauty and conveniently small size.

Palma de Sierra

(Palma Barrigona de Sierra)
Gaussia princeps H. Wendl.

Family: Arecaceae (Palmae)

Origin: Cuba (endemic).

Height: Up to 15 m (50 ft) tall.

Trunk: Solitary, slender and straight, slightly swollen at the base, with smooth grey bark.

Canopy: A pinnate palm with few leaves.

Leaves: Feathery, pale green, up to 2.5 m (8 ft) long. Only five or six leaves appear on the tree at any one time; they bear long, pointed leaflets about 35 cm (14 in) long.

Flowers: Inconspicuous, appearing in short clumps on long, slender stalks below the leaves.

Fruit: An elliptical single-seeded drupe 1 cm (about ½ in) long, which turns reddish-orange as it ripens.

Comments: This graceful palm grows profusely, with its woody roots exposed, from the karst cliffs that form the vertical slopes of the 'mogotes' of the province of Pinar del Río. It is never seen in the flatter areas of the province, but is successfully cultivated in botanical gardens.

Palma Petate

(Crinita, Guano Barudo, Petate)
Coccothrinax crinita Becc. subsp. *crinita*

Family: Arecaceae (Palmae)

Origin: Cuba, endemic.

Height: Up to 10 m (33ft) tall in very old specimens.

Trunk: Completely covered with long, light brown hairs in young palms; the trunk is cylindrical and smooth in old ones and measures about 20 cm (8 in) in diameter.

Canopy: A palmate palm, with a densely leafed crown.

Leaves: Circular, 1 m (3¼ ft) or more in diameter, with about 55 segments deeply divided halfway to the base, split at the tips, glossy green above and greyish below.

Flowers: Very tiny, creamy white, growing upwards when young and pendent at maturity, in racemes of 80–100 cm (32–40 in) or more in length, growing among the leaves. Blossoms June to August.

Fruit: 2 cm (¾ in) in diameter, pink to purple, becoming almost black when fully ripe, in erect racemes. The single seed is round, creamy white, wrinkled on the surface and about 15 mm (½ in) in diameter.

Comments: This is a remarkable palm, with its profusely bearded trunk and its large, round, shiny leaves. It only occurs naturally at Bahía Honda in the province of Pinar del Río, where it appears in secondary semi-deciduous forests, as well as beside rivers. Only around a hundred mature trees now remain, for in the past these palms used to be felled for numerous practical purposes: the fibres were used for making pillows and mattresses, the leaves for hats and brooms, and the highly durable trunks for rural buildings. Forest fires further aggravated the situation, and now the Palma Petate has been declared as critically endangered, a situation that the Cuban National Botanic Garden is currently attempting to reverse.

Palma Real

(Royal Palm, Cuban Royal Palm)
Roystonea regia ((Kunth) O.F. Cook)

Synonym: *Oreodoxa regia* Kunth

Family: Palmae (Arecaceae)

Origin: Cuba, Florida (USA).

Height: Up to 25 m (80 ft) in good soil conditions.

Trunk: Swollen at the base and in the middle; smooth, grey, slightly ringed, the surface often speckled with spots of lichen; maximum diameter about 85 cm (34 in).

Canopy: Pinnate palm.

Leaves: The terminal crown is formed of 12 to 15 feathery, bright green leaves about 3 m (10 ft) long, with two rows of hundreds of leaflets along the two sides of the central axis. The crownshaft is long and pale green.

Flowers: The huge bunches which appear just below the crownshaft are profusely branched and bear thousands of tiny creamy-white flowers almost all year round.

Fruit: Reddish-purple, 10–15 mm (about ½ in) long, 5–10 mm (¼–½ in) wide, single seeded.

Comments: Cuban national tree. Naturally widespread all over the country in plains, hills up to 800 m (2 625 ft) above sea level and along rivers, in fertile and well-drained soil. The tree is used extensively by country people: the wood for furniture and housing, the leaves for thatching and basketry, the seeds for pig feed and oil production. The crownshaft is used to wrap dried tobacco leaves before shipping.

Palo Balsa

(Lanero, Balsa Tree)
Ochroma pyramidale (Cav. ex Lam.) Urb.

Synonym: *Ochroma lagopus* Sw.

Family: Malvaceae (formerly Bombacaceae)

Origin: New World Tropics.

Height: Up to 30 m (100 ft).

Trunk: Cylindrical, with a smooth brown surface; up to 60 cm (24 in) diameter.

Canopy: Oblong, compact.

Leaves: Heart-shaped or with three to five small lobes; very variable in dimensions; green on the upper surface, grey with brown veins beneath.

Flowers: Single, ivory-coloured flowers, calyx cup-shaped, corolla with five large petals; the tree flowers from November to March.

Fruit: The seed pod is brown and woody with a woolly surface; it contains small seeds among further woolly filaments. When the pod opens, the seeds disperse along with the filaments of wool.

Comments: The wood of this tree is light and porous and its trunk floats well in salt and fresh water; the Spanish word for 'raft' is 'balsa'. The wood was used by the famous Norwegian scientist Thor Heyerdahl in the construction of the raft 'Kon Tiki', on which he voyaged from South America to the Pacific islands. It also used to be used for aircraft construction because of its light weight. Palo Balsa is considered a Cuban native tree, but its presence in the tropical forests of Baracoa in the extreme east of the island may be due to early introduction by Arawak Indians from South America, where they used it for the construction of canoes. Nowadays it may also be found at Santo Domingo, in the mountains of the Sierra Maestra.

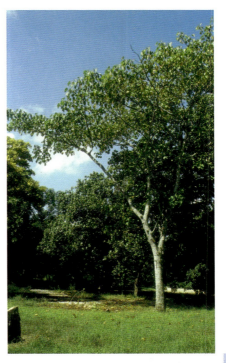

Palo Bobo

(Botija, Brazilian Rose, Silk Cotton, Buttercup Tree)
Cochlospermum vitifolium (Willd.) Spreng.

Family: Cochlospermaceae

Origin: Central and South America.

Height: A small tree 5–12 m (16–40 ft) high.

Trunk: Stout, with grey bark.

Canopy: Rounded, very open, deciduous.

Leaves: Alternate; the five-lobed leaves look like hands. Each of the lobes has a sharp tip, the bases are heart-shaped and the edges are serrated. The entire leaf is 10–30 cm (4–12 in) wide and deep green in colour. The tree sheds its leaves in December and the new shoots appear in April.

Flowers: Very attractive, grouped in terminal clusters of large, brilliant, silky, yellow rose-like flowers with numerous

petals and stamens, measuring 10–12 cm (4–5 in) across. Blossoms in February to March.

Fruit: The dark brown five-valved seed pod 7–8 cm (about 3 in) across is filled with silky cotton fibres attached to the seeds. It is easy to produce new plants from large cuttings.

Comments: Palo Bobo is a beautiful native flowering tree used as an ornamental in open spaces; it is also used to create hedges. The fibre found in the fruits is used for stuffing pillows.

Paraíso

(Indian Lilac, Pride of India)
Melia azedarach L.

WARNING: The fruits are poisonous.

Family: Meliaceae

Origin: India.

Height: About 15 m (50 ft).

Trunk: Often straight, with rough brown bark, about 80 cm (32 in) in diameter when the tree is very old.

Canopy: Rounded with light foliage.

Leaves: Grouped at the end of branches, compound, formed of numerous leaflets with serrated edges, light green. About 70 cm (28 in) long.

Flowers: The fragrant, attractive mauve flowers appear grouped in small bunches. Blossoms during the dry season, from November to January.

Fruit: Oval, yellow, with a smooth surface; 2–4 cm (¾–1½ in) long. Poisonous to humans.

Comments: Paraíso is a popular, fast-growing, ornamental tree. It is naturalized in Cuba. The wood is used for furniture and sculpture and the branches and leaves are recommended for purifying baths by the devotees of Afro-Cuban religious cults. Paraíso is sometimes confused with the closely related species *Azadirachta indica*, known as the Nim Tree, although the canopy of the latter is much more dense.

Pimienta

(Pimienta de Jamaica, Allspice)
Pimenta dioica (L.) Merr.

Family: Myrtaceae

Origin: Cuba, Jamaica, Yucatán (México).

Height: 10–15 m (33–50 ft).

Trunk: Straight with pale brown bark.

Canopy: Rounded, leafy, perennial.

Leaves: Alternate, elliptical with a notched apex, dark green, 6–14 cm (2¼–5½ in) long. The leaves have a strong, spicy scent.

Flowers: The sexes are separated in different plants. The small, white flowers, which smell strongly of spice, appear in racemes; they bear four sepals and four petals, and the male flower has numerous stamens. Blossoms in summer.

Fruit: A small spherical black berry 4–6 mm (about ¼ in) in diameter containing one or two seeds, with a strong spicy flavour.

Comments: Pimienta is the tree which produces Allspice, which is extensively used for culinary purposes; it owes this name to the manner in which it combines the flavours of nutmeg, cloves and cinnamon. The tree is widely cultivated in other Caribbean islands but is comparatively rare in Cuba. The spice is produced by drying and grinding the unripe berries. Pimienta can be found naturalized in Cuba's eastern rain forests, and is also a native of the Cabo Cruz area.

Pino Macho

(Pine Tree, Caribbean Pine)
Pinus caribaea Morelet var. *caribaea*

Family: Pinaceae

Origin: Cuba; other varieties of pine occur in Central America and the Bahamas.

Height: Up to 30 m (100 ft).

Trunk: Simple, straight, cylindrical; with very flaky bark.

Canopy: A typical conical canopy in young trees.

Leaves: Needles, growing in short branches in groups of three, about 20 cm (8 in) long and 1–2 mm (less than 1/10 in) wide, very hard.

Flowers: The tree does not bear true flowers; the reproductive structure is a cone in which are contained sacs of pollen that looks like fine, bright yellow dust. The female cone is brown and woody and bears the ovules. The pollen is borne from tree to tree by the wind.

Fruit: Pino Macho does bear true fruits; the winged seeds are contained within the female cone, which opens when ripe to release the seeds.

Comments: This is a very useful tree: the timber is used for furniture and construction and the aromatic resin is used in the pharmaceutical and paint industries. The seeds are edible.

Piñón

(Piñón de Pito, Piñón de Cerca, Piñón de Sombra, Búcare, Indian Coral Tree, Coral Bean, Cockspur)
Erythrina spp.

WARNING: The majority of the species have sharp spines.

Family: Leguminosae (Fabaceae)

Origin: Tropical regions of the world.

Height: Varies according to the species; some of these trees grow to prodigious heights.

Trunk: Usually thick; always profusely branched.

Canopy: Deciduous, rounded.

Leaves: Alternate, compound of three leaflets, that at the end being larger than the two opposite one another; variably sized; medium to deep green above and paler below.

Flowers: Large and showy, in terminal or axillary racemes of pyramidal shape. The flowers are bright red or orange, almost tubular, of variable size according to the species and frequently appear before the new leaves, during the dry season.

Fruit: The thin, bean-like seed pod looks rather like a necklace. The seed pods are red to brown and measure 10–20 cm (4–8 in) long. The seeds are almost spherical. These plants are easily propagated from large cuttings.

Comments: This is a genus with more than a hundred species in both the New and the Old Worlds. They are frequently used as ornamentals, or as shade trees for coffee and cocoa plantations, as well as for hedging.

Reina de las Flores

(Júpiter de la Reina, Queen of Flowers, Pride of India)
Lagerstroemia speciosa (L.) Pers.

Family: Lythraceae

Origin: Tropical Asia.

Height: A medium-sized tree that can grow to 15 m (50 ft).

Trunk: Straight, light brown, smooth.

Canopy: Rounded, leafy. The tree is deciduous.

Leaves: Growing alternately from the stem, elliptical to spear-shaped with sharp tips, dull green above and paler green below with yellow veining; up to 15–20 cm (6–8 in) long and 5–6 cm (just over 2 in) wide.

Flowers: Very attractive, appearing in large numbers in generous, light grey terminal panicles of pale pink flowers that fade to dark pink during the day. The flowers have a cup-shaped, pale grey, slightly hairy calyx with six star-like lobes; the corolla has six curled petals and a very narrow base, and numerous pink stamens appear at the centre of the flower, which measures approximately 8 cm (3 in) in diameter. Blossoms from May to August.

Comments: This is a spectacular tree when it is in flower, with an outstanding display of different tones of pink in its large clusters of blossom. In its region of origin the wood is highly prized for its quality, being used for boat construction, furniture, flooring, etc.

Fruit: The spherical, woody, brown seed pod of 2–3 cm (about 1 in) in diameter opens in six to seven parts to release the small winged seeds.

Roble Amarillo

(Yellow Poui)
Tabebuia chrysantha (Jacq.) G. Nicholson

Family: Bignoniaceae

Origin: Tropical America.

Height: Up to 15 m (50 ft) tall, less in Cuba.

Trunk: Straight, with furrowed, light brown bark.

Canopy: Rounded–narrow; deciduous.

Leaves: Alternate, compound, with five to seven large leaflets 15–25 cm (6–10 in) long suspended from long petioles, light green with coppery fur on both sides; this fur also appears on new growth and on the petioles.

Flowers: Highly attractive; the clusters of numerous golden-yellow flowers grow from the ends of the branches and twigs. They are trumpet-shaped, about 6–7 cm (2½ in) long and wide with five lobes with frilled edges. The flowers appear before the growth of leaves, in March to April.

Fruit: The hanging, brown seed pod that is up to 40 cm (16 in) long opens longitudinally when ripe to permit the dispersal of the winged seeds by the wind.

Comments: This is one of the most beautiful flowering trees in the Caribbean: it is a blaze of golden-yellow blossom when in flower. The Roble Amarillo is the Venezuelan national tree.

Roble de Yugo

(Roble Blanco)
Tabebuia angustata Britton

Family: Bignoniaceae

Origin: Cuba, Jamaica.

Height: Up to 12 m (40 ft).

Trunk: Straight, about 35 cm (14 in) in diameter; the furrowed bark is brown with grey patches.

Canopy: Narrow, sparse.

Leaves: Deciduous, alternate, made up of three to seven finger-shaped leaflets. The leaf as a whole is 5–18 cm (2–7 in) long, bright green, stiff and spear-shaped, with a leathery surface and a sharp tip.

Flowers: Highly attractive, appearing after the leaves have fallen, in clusters of up to 40 pale pink, white or mauve flowers growing at the ends of the branches and twigs. The individual flowers are 7 cm (2¾ in) long and 7 cm (2¾ in) wide and asymmetrically trumpet-shaped, with yellow throats and five lobes that are frilled at the edges. Blossoms May to June.

Fruit: A long, brown seed pod 10–25 cm (4–10 in) long, which opens when ripe to release the seeds.

Comments: Roble de Yugo is a beautiful native tree common on the banks of rivers and creeks, in swamps and in woods at lower altitudes. Its timber is used for making tools. It is also popular as an ornamental because of its beautiful pale-pink blossoms; it may be seen throughout the city of Havana.

Roble Guayo

(Guayo Prieto, Bastard Stopper, Fiddle Wood)
Petitia domingensis Jacq.

Family: Lamiaceae

Origin: West Indies.

Height: Up to 22 m (72 ft), commonly less.

Trunk: Straight, thick, smooth, with peeling bark.

Canopy: Rounded with dense foliage, perennial.

Leaves: Growing opposite one another from the angular twigs, with long stalks, the leaves are oval with sharp tips, dull green above and yellow-green, furry and with prominent veins below, 6–10 cm (2¼–4 in) long.

Flowers: Tiny, white, numerous on long panicles hanging from angular stems growing in the axils of the leaves. Very fragrant.

Fruit: In racemes of numerous red, rounded fleshy fruits of about 5 mm (¼ in). These little 'grapes' turn black when very ripe.

Comments: Roble Guayo is commonly found in dry woodlands and on chalky soil. Its wood is hard and heavy.

Roble Maquiligua

(Roble Magriña, Pink Poui, Pink Tecoma, White Cedar, Pink Trumpet Tree)
Tabebuia heterophylla (DC.) Britton

Synonym: *Tabebuia pentaphylla* (L.) Hemsl.

Family: Bignoniaceae

Origin: Tropical America.

Height: Up to 18 m (60 ft) high, usually less in Cuba.

Trunk: Light brown, up to 60 cm (24 in) diameter, slightly rough.

Canopy: Open.

Leaves: Alternate, compound with two to five leaflets forming leaves looking rather like an open hand, vary widely in shape and size, bright green above and paler below.

Flowers: The trumpet-shaped pink flowers, which appear when the tree is leafless, are arranged in bunches of numerous (35–40) blooms 7–10 cm (2¾–4 in) long. Blossoms erratically from April to August.

Fruit: The long seed pod, which measures about 20 cm long by 6 mm wide (8 by ¼ in), opens when ripe to permit the dispersal of the winged seeds.

Comments: This magnificent tree was introduced into Cuba from Mexico and Central America during the first half of the twentieth century. Fallen blossoms often cause the ground surrounding the tree to look like a pink carpet. In other countries, its wood is used for furniture and the trees are planted for shade on coffee plantations.

Roble Vitex

Vitex parviflora Juss.

Family: Lamiaceae

Origin: Tropical Asia.

Height: Up to 15 m (50 ft) tall.

Trunk: Straight, slender, light brown.

Canopy: Rounded, dense, with right-angled twigs.

Leaves: Perennial, opposite, with long petioles. Formed of three large elliptical lobes with sharp tips and undulating edges, dull green above and paler below, with a yellow central vein; the entire leaf is 15–30 cm (6–12 in) long.

Flowers: Delicate, in terminal and axillary clusters 23–24 cm (about 9 in) long of numerous small, pale blue-violet flowers, each of which has a cup-shaped calyx and a tubular corolla terminating in five lobes, the upper one wider and more brightly coloured than the others, with closely grouped stamens rising from the two lower lobes. Blossoms during the rainy season; the flowers are subtly scented.

Fruit: A purplish-black, spherical drupe 8–10 mm (3/10–4/10 in) in diameter.

Comments: Roble Vitex is commonly used as an ornamental tree in parks and avenues in the city of Havana for its delicate, fragrant flowers and its perennial foliage.

Salvadera

(Habana, Habilla, Sand Box Tree, Monkey Pistol)
Hura crepitans L.

WARNING: The milky sap of this tree, and its seeds, are extremely poisonous.

Family: Euphorbiaceae

Origin: Mexico.

Height: Up to 20 m (65 ft).

Trunk: Straight, wide, light brown, spiny.

Canopy: Rounded, densely leafy.

Leaves: Alternate, heart-shaped with sharp tips, from 6–18 cm (2¼–7 in) long, bright green.

Flowers: Both genders of flower grow on the same tree. The female flowers are inconspicuous, of a dull red colour; the male flowers are tiny in spikes of 3–5 cm (1–2 in), on a stalk 5–11 cm (2–4½ in) long. Blooms from April to June.

Fruit: A round capsule of about 8 cm (3 in) diameter divided into numerous sections containing one seed each. When the capsule is very dry it explodes noisily, dispersing the flat seeds to a considerable distance from the tree.

Comments: Salvadera is not native to Cuba. It is usually planted for shade in parks and on roadsides. Its milky sap is extremely harmful to the skin and eyes, and the seeds are poisonous.

Triplaris

(Palo Hormiguero)
Triplaris americana L.

Family: Polygonaceae

Origin: Central America.

Height: Up to 20 m (65 ft); in Cuba usually lower.

Trunk: Straight, with no branches growing from the lower part. The bark, grey mottled with brown, is papery and peels off in strips.

Canopy: Almost vertical, with short branches.

Leaves: Large, up to 30 cm (12 in) long, elliptical in shape, deep green on both sides. Triplaris is a perennial tree.

Flowers: The male and female flowers are separated between different trees. The male ones are very small, attached to branching spikes at the end of the twigs; they are greenish-white and strongly scented. The female tree also bears small flowers in terminal spikes. Their small pink sepals are late to appear and thus remain attached to the fruit. The female flower is not scented. Blossoms in January to early March.

Fruit: Very attractive, in bunches at the end of the twigs; the attached pinkish-red sepals expand to form wings for a small parachute structure.

Comments: It is the spectacular fruit rather than the flower of Triplaris that provides its decorative allure. Although it is a very attractive and fast-growing tree, it is not very commonly planted in Cuba. Its common name, 'Palo Hormiguero', alludes to the fact that ants tend to colonize the tree in the Central American countries from which it originated.

Tulipán Africano

(Espatodea, African Tulip Tree, Tulip Tree)
Spathodea campanulata Beauv.

WARNING: The fruits of this tree are poisonous.

Family: Bignoniaceae

Origin: Tropical Africa.

Height: 15–25 m (50–80 ft).

Trunk: Straight, smooth, grey, up to 40 cm (16 in) in diameter.

Canopy: Oval shape.

Leaves: Large, up to 60 cm (24 in) long, compound of four to eight pairs of leaflets, deep olive green. Perennial.

Flowers: Very showy; asymmetrical bell-shaped flowers up to 12 cm (5 in) long grouped in circular racemes at the ends of the branches outside the canopy; scarlet to orange. The unopened flower buds contain liquid.

Fruit: The pods are 20 cm (8 in) long and contain winged seeds; the fruit is extremely poisonous.

Comments: This beautiful ornamental tree may be seen all over Cuba. It was introduced into the island at the beginning of the twentieth century by the Experimental Agronomic Station and has become naturalized growing widely on plains and in the mountains, mainly in the Western provinces.

Uva Caleta

(Uvero, Sea Grape, Shore Grape, Seaside Grape)
Coccoloa uvifera L.

Family: Polygonaceae

Origin: West Indies, Florida (USA), Bahamas and Caribbean coasts of Central and South America.

Height: Shrub or tree 2–5 m (6½–17 ft) tall.

Trunk: Variable diameter, smooth with patches of light green, grey and salmon on its bark; numerous branches.

Canopy: Extended, the shape being dependent upon the force and direction of continuous sea breezes.

Leaves: Alternate, with reddish petioles, rounded or kidney-shaped, 6–13 cm (2¼–5 in) long and 8–18 cm (3–7 in) wide; the reddish veins are prominent in both sides. The new leaves are bronze-coloured and the old ones turn red before falling from the tree. They have a waxy appearance.

Flowers: Tiny, densely arranged in slender, creamy-white spikes 15–20 cm (6–8 in) long, arising from the axils of the leaves. Blossoms April to May. The flowers are scented and attract large quantities of bees.

Fruit: A cluster of round 'grapes' which turn from light green to dark purple when ripe.

Comments: This tree is popular for its sweet grape-like fruit and the shade it provides on the beach. The wood is pink, hard and compact. Uva Caleta forms the so-called 'uverales' – bands of woody vegetation along the sandy shoreline, together with 'Guano de Costa' (*Thrinax radiata*) and 'Icaco' (*Chrysobalanos icaco*). The fruit of Uva Caleta is used for making wine and puddings.

Varía

(Baría, Varía Negra, Varía Prieta, Spanish Elm, Panichellum)
Cordia gerascanthus L.

Family: Boraginaceae

Origin: Central America and the Caribbean.

Height: A tall tree, which has been known to reach a height of 20 m (65 ft).

Trunk: Straight, with furrowed, light brown bark.

Canopy: The perennial canopy is narrow and dense.

Leaves: Alternate, dark green leaves, spear-shaped with sharp tips, 5–12 cm (2–5 in) long.

Flowers: Very attractive, in dense clusters of fragrant white blossoms with a tubular corolla terminating in five rounded lobes 2–3 cm (¾–1 in) long, fading to a papery pale brown when mature and remaining

attached to the tree for some time. Blossoms in March to May.

Fruit: Dry seed pods to which the papery petals remain attached, performing the function of wings for wind dispersal.

Comments: Varía is one of the most beautiful Cuban native trees. It is frequently used in streets (a particularly attractive example may be seen in 23rd Street in Havana) and parks. The Varía tree is resistant to drought, as its natural habitat is the dry coastal forest of Cuba.

Vomitel Colorado

(Vomitel, Geiger Tree, Scarlet Cordia, Anaconda, Geranium Tree)
Cordia sebestena L.

Family: Boraginaceae

Origin: Tropical America.

Height: A perennial shrub or small tree growing up to 8 m (26 ft) high.

Trunk: Slender, with smooth, dark brown bark.

Canopy: Rounded and dense.

Leaves: The alternate leaves are of a rounded oval shape with pointed tips. They have a rough surface texture, and are dark, dull green above and pale green on their lower surfaces. They measure 9–16 cm (3½–6½ in) long and 5–14 cm (2–5½ in) wide.

Flowers: Attractive, in rounded terminal clusters of about 10 to 15 flowers each; bright red-orange, trumpet-shaped, terminating in six round, flat lobes measuring 2.5 cm (1 in) across. Blossoms during the rainy season.

Fruit: Fleshy, white, plum-like fruits of about 2.5 cm (1 in) in diameter; fragrant and sweet, with one to three seeds.

Comments: Vomitel Colorado is a small but beautiful perennial native tree, frequently planted as an ornamental. It occurs naturally in coastal vegetation and is thus resistant to drought. Its fruits may be eaten either raw or cooked, but they are not particularly tasty. Its wood is used for fine furniture and musical instruments.

Yagruma

(Yagruma Hembra, Snake Wood, Trumpet Tree)
Cecropia peltata L.

Family: Moraceae (Cecropiaceae)

Origin: Tropical America.

Height: Up to 20 m (65 ft).

Trunk: Straight, slender, grey, often covered in rows of little holes made by woodpeckers.

Canopy: Extended but with widely spaced branches.

Leaves: Growing alternately from the twigs, very large, divided to about halfway down the body of the leaf into seven to nine lobes, dull dark green with a rough texture above and grey, soft and furry beneath, with a long, rounded, hollow petiole. The leaf is 30–50 cm (12–20 in) in diameter.

Flowers: Minute, inconspicuous flowers appear in gender-separated spikes. Blossoms sporadically all year round.

Fruit: Very small with tiny seeds which appear en masse like powder.

Comments: Yagruma is a common native tree, growing profusely in woods all over the island. It is planted as an ornamental for its large, attractive leaves, which are also used for flower arrangements when they have fallen and dried into curly shapes. The leaves are also renowned as a remedy for asthma relief. The trunk and the petioles are hollow and the holes made by woodpeckers in the trunk of the Yagruma are usually full of little insects that serve as food for other birds.

Yarey Hembra

Copernicia baileyana León

Family: Palmae (Arecaceae)

Origin: Cuba, endemic.

Height: 10–15 m (33–50 ft).

Trunk: Very large (about 60 cm [24 in] diameter), spindle-shaped, greyish-white, smooth.

Canopy: A palmate palm.

Leaves: Looking rather like giant, glossy green fans, the leaves of Yarey Hembra are wedge-shaped and can grow to up to 2 m (6½ ft) long; the petiole is enlarged at the base and edged with sharp teeth. The leaves grow upright and are divided from a quarter of the way to the base into numerous segments, the outer of which are toothed; the segments begin to droop as the leaves age.

Flowers: The small, creamy-white flowers appear in extremely long (3 m [10 ft]), arching, branched spadices growing beyond the canopy and among the leaves. Blossoms in June to August.

Fruit: The rounded, brown drupe contains one seed, of about 2 cm (¾ in) diameter.

Comments: Yarey Hembra is one of the most impressive Cuban palms, surpassed only by *Copernicia fallaensis*, a blue-green leafed species also known as Yarey. Yarey Hembra is found in the Central and Eastern provinces of Cuba, in savannas and flood forests. Its leaves are used to make hats and craft items, and for the thatching of houses.

Glossary

Alternate: describes leaves alternating up a stem, growing first on one side then the other.
Aril: a fleshy mass of tissue covering a seed.
Axil: the upper angle between a leaf and a stem.
Axillary: growing from an axil.
Bract: a leaf or scale below the calyx.
Calyx: the whorl of leaves forming the outer case of a bud or envelope of a flower.
Canopy: the branches and foliage of a tree.
Capsule: a dry seed-case opening when ripe by parting of valves.
Compound leaf: a leaf formed by sub-units known as 'leaflets'.
Corolla: the whorl of modified leaves known as petals, separate or joined, forming the inner envelope of a flower.
Costapalmate: a palm leaf in which the petiole projects well into the leaf blade, curving downwards.
Crownshaft: the columnar structure, composed of interlocking leaf bases, that completely envelops the bud at the apex of the trunk of a palm.
Dehisce: burst open.
Drupe: a fleshy or pulpy fruit enclosing a stone or nut with a kernel.
Endemic: applied to a species or group of organisms which occur naturally in a restricted geographical region.
Epiphyte: a plant that grows naturally upon another plant but does not derive any nourishment from it.
Gymnosperms: plant having seeds unprotected by fruit.
Inflorescence: the complete flower head of a plant.
Karst: limestone/associated mineral processes.
Leaflet: one of the parts of which a compound leaf is composed.
Mogotes: small rounded limestone 'mountains' that remained when surrounding rocks were dissolved by water over millions of years.
Obovate: ovate with a narrower end at the base.
Ovate: egg-shaped.
Ovule: a female egg cell.
Palmate: used to describe a leaf with segments radiating from a central point; having lobes like spread fingers.
Panicle: a loose, irregular type of compound inflorescence.
Pedicel: the stalk of a flower in an inflorescence.
Perennial: a plant that lives for more than two years.
Petiole: a slender stalk joining the leaf-blade to the stem.
Pinna: a unit (leaflet) of a compound leaf.
Pinnate: with a series of leaflets on each side of a common petiole.
Pistil: the female parts of a flower.
Raceme: a type of inflorescence in which the flowers are arranged along an axis.
Rhizome: a horizontal underground stem that bears small roots.
Semi-deciduous: used to describe a (wood or) forest in which approximately half the trees lose their leaves during the dry season.
Sepal: modified leaves that form the calyx of a flower.
Sheath: the lowest part of the petiole, enveloping the stem.
Spadice: a type of inflorescence in which the central flower is covered by a modified leaf known as the spathe.
Spike: a type of inflorescence in which a long stem bears many stalkless flowers.
Stamen: the male organ of a flower, composed of a filament and anther.
Style: a part of the female organs of the flower.
Terminal: at the end or tip.
Whorl: a ring of leaves or other organs around the stem.

Bibliography

Alain, Hno [Liogier, H.A.] (1974) *Flora de Cuba. Suplemento*. Instituto Cubano del Libro, Editorial Organismos, La Habana.

Barwick, M. (2004) *Tropical and Subtropical Trees: An Encyclopedia*. Timber Press, Portland.

Bisse, J. (1988) *Arboles de Cuba*. Editorial Científico-Ténica, La Habana.

Borhidi, A. (1991) *Phytogeography and Vegetation Ecology of Cuba*. Akadémiai Kiadó, Budapest.

Clement, I.D., Clement, V.W., Walsingham, F.G., Weeks, J.W. & Weeks, K.C. (1954) *Guide to the Most Interesting Plants of the Atkins Garden*. Harvard University, Atkins Garden and Laboratory, Cienfuegos.

García, R. *et al*. (1997) *Importancia de las plantas nativas y endémicas en la reforestación*. Editorial Corripio, Santo Domingo.

Howard, R.A. (1988–1989) *Flora of the Lesser Antilles, Leeward and Windward Islands*. Arnold Arboretum of Harvard University, Jamaica Plain, Massachusetts.

Jones, D.L. (1984) *Palms of Australia*. Reed Books Pty Ltd, French Forests, New South Wales.

Leiva, A. (1999) *Las palmas en Cuba*. Editorial Científico-Técnica, La Habana.

Lennox, G.W. & Seddon, S.A. (1978) *Flowers of the Caribbean*. Macmillan Education, London.

León, Hno & Alain, Hno [Liogier, H.A.] (1946–1957) *Flora de Cuba*. Contribuciónes Ocasional Museo de Natural Historia Colegio de La Salle 8, 10, 13, 16.

McCurrach, J.C. (1960) *Palms of the World*. 1980 reprint by Horticultural Books, Florida.

Roig y Mesa, J.T. (1963) *Diccionario botánico de nombres vulgares cubanos*, 3rd edn, 1–2. Editorial Científico-Técnica, La Habana.

Roig y Mesa, J.T. (1974) *Plantas medicinales, aromáticas o venenosas de Cuba*, 2nd edn. Editorial Científico-Técnica, La Habana.

Royal Botanic Gardens Kew (1997) *Index Kewensis 2.0 [CD-ROM]*. Oxford University Press, Oxford.

Scurlock, J. P. (1987) *Native Trees and Shrubs of the Florida Keys. A Field Guide*. Laurel & Hebert, Inc, Lower Sugarloaf Key, Florida.

Seddon, S.A. & Lennox, G.W. (1980) *Trees of the Caribbean*. Macmillan Education, London.

Sosa, V. & Flores, J.S. (1993) *La flora ornamental de Mérida*. Ayuntamiento de Mérida, Yucatán.

Various (1998–2003) *Flora de la República de Cuba*. Koeltz Scientific Books, Germany.

Vázquez, C., Figueroa, V. & Lamas, J. (2004) *Las plantas de nuestro Huerto. 3. Frutales y sus recetas*. Editorial Proyecto Comunitario de Conservación de Alimentos, La Habana.

Zulueta, M.E. & Moreno, H. (eds) (1999) *Cuba y sus árboles*. Editorial Academia & Caja Madrid, La Habana & Madrid.

Index of Common Names

Abrojo (de la Florida), 1
Achiote, 20
Adonidia, 2
Aguacate, 3
Aguacate cimarrón, 4
Aguedita, 5
Alamo de la India, 6
Algarrobo (del país), 7
Algarrobo de olor, 8
Allspice, 84
Almácigo (azucarero/Colorado), 9
Almendra (almond), 10
Anacagüita, 11
Apple blossom cassia, 29
Araucaria, 12
Arbol de las salchichas, 13
Arbol del nim, 14
Arbol del pan, 15
Arbol del viajero, 16
Australian pine, 30
Autograph tree, 38
Avocado, 3

Bacona, 17
Bagá, 18
Balsa tree, 81
Balsam fig, 38
Barrigona (de Vueltabajo), 72
Bastard cedar, 51
Bastard stopper, 90
Bella hortensia, 1
Bienvestido, 19
Bija, 20
Bitter bush, 5
Bitterwood, 47
Blue mahoe, 64
Bottlebrush tree, 22
Breadfruit, 15
Buccaneer palm, 77
Buttercup tree, 82
Butterfly tree, 70

Cabbage palm, 73
Cacao, 21
Calabash tree, 54
Calistemon, 22
Cañafístola, 23

Cañandonga, 24
Candlenut, 68
Capberry sweetwood, 35
Carambola, 26
Cardenal, 27
Caribbean pine, 85
Carolina, 28
Casia nodosa (de Java), 29
Casuarina, 30
Cedro (cedar), 31
Ceiba (ceibo), 32
Ceibon, 33
Cheflera, 34
Chinese fan palm, 74
Chocolate tree, 21
Cigua, 35
Cockspur, 86
Coco plumoso, 36
Cocoa, 21
Coconut palm, 37
Cocotero, 37
Copey, 38
Coral shower, 24
Corcho, 76
Corojo (espinoso), 39
Cuba bark, 64
Cuban petticoat palm, 57

Dagame, 40
Drago, 33
Dwarf date palm, 42

Encina (encino), 41

Fenix robelín, 42
Ficus lira, 43
Fiddle wood, 90
Fiddle-leaf fig, 43
Flamboyant, 44
Flame tree, 44
Framboyán, 44
Framboyán amarillo, 45
Frangipán (frangipani), 62
Frijolillo, 46

Gavilán, 47
Geiger tree, 98
Geranium tree, 98

Golden cane palm, 71
Golden fig, 56
Guana, 48
Guano de costa, 49
Guao, 50
Guásima, 51
Guasimilla, 52
Guava, 53
Guayaba, 53
Güira, 54

Horse cassia, 24

Indian coral tree, 86
Indian laburnum, 23
Indian lilac, 83

Jagua, 55
Jagüey hembra, 56
Jaimiqui, 17
Jata de guanabacoa, 57
Jocuma, 58
Jubabán, 59
Júcaro, 60
Jungle plum, 58

Kapok, 32

Lancewood, 35
Laurel de la India, 61
Lirio (de costa/tricolor), 62

Magnolia, 63
Mahogany, 25
Majagua (azul), 64
Mamey Colorado, 65
Mango, 66
Manilla palm, 2
Marmalade box, 55
Miraguano, 67
Monkey pistol, 93
Mother-in-law's tongue, 8
Mountain mahoe, 64

Neem (nim), 14
Nodding cassia, 29
Nogal de la India, 68
Norfolk Island pine, 12

103

Oak, 41
Octopus tree, 34
Ocuje, 69
Orchid tree, 70
Orquídea silvestre, 70

Pagoda tree, 62
Palma areca, 71
Palma barrigona, 72
Palma cana, 73
Palma de abanico, 74
Palma de alcanfor (sagú), 75
Palma de corcho, 76
Palma de Santa Lucía (Guinea), 77
Palma de Sierra, 78
Palma petate, 79
Palma real, 80
Palmetto palm, 73
Palo balsa, 81
Paradise tree, 47
Paraíso, 83
Pea tree, 19
Peaberry palm, 49
Pimienta (de Jamaica), 84
Pine tree, 85
Pink poui (tecoma/trumpet tree), 91
Pino macho, 85
Piñón (de pito/cerca/sombra), 86
Poinciana, 44

Pond apple, 18
Pride of Guatemala, 27
Pride of India, 83, 87

Queen of flowers, 87
Queen palm, 36
Quick stick, 19

Reina de las flores, 87
Roble amarillo, 88
Roble de Yugo (blanco), 89
Roble Guayo, 90
Roble Maquiligua (Magriña), 91
Roble vitex, 92
Royal palm, 80

Sacred fig, 6
Sago palm, 75
Salvadera, 93
Saman, 7
Sand box tree, 93
Sausage tree, 13
Scarlet cordia, 98
Sea (shore) grape, 96
Shaving brush tree, 28
Shower of gold, 23
Silk cotton, 82
Snake wood, 99
Spanish elm, 97
Star fruit, 26
Strangler fig, 56

Sweet torchwood, 35

Temple tree, 62
Thatch palm, 49
Traveller's palm, 16
Triplaris, 94
Tropical almond, 10
Trumpet tree, 99
Tulip tree, 95
Tulipán Africano, 95

Ulvero, 96
Umbrella tree, 34
Uva caleta, 96

Varnish tree, 68
Vomitel Colorado, 98

Walnut, 68
Weeping fig, 61
West Indian birch, 9
White cedar, 91
Wild fig, 56
Wild mahogany, 59
Wild olive, 58

Yagruma (hembra), 99
Yarey hembra, 100
Yellow flamboyant, 45
Yellow poui, 88
Yuraguana, 67

Index of Scientific Names

Adonidia merrillii. See
   Veitchia merrillii
Albizia cubana, 17
   lebbek, 8
Aleurites moluccana, 68
   triloba, 68
Annona glabra, 18
   palustris, 18
Araucaria heterophylla, 12
Arecastrum romanzoffianum.
   See *Syagrus romanzoffiana*
Artocarpus altilis, 15
   communis, 15
Averhoa carambola, 26
Azadirachta indica, 14

Bauhinia spp., 70
Belotia grewiaefolia. See
   Trichospermum mexicanum
Bixa orellana, 20
Bombacopsis cubensis, 33
Bombax ellipticum. See
   Pseudobombax ellipticum
Brassaia actinophylla, 34
Bucida subinermis, 60
Bursera simarouba, 9

Callistemon speciosus, 22
Calophyllum antillanum, 69
   brasiliense var. *antillanum*, 69
Calycophyllum candidissimum, 40
Cassia fistula, 23
   grandis, 24
   javanica, 29
   nodosa, 29
Casuarina equisetifolia, 30
Cecropia peltata, 99
Cedrela mexicana, 31
   odorata, 31
Ceiba pentandra, 32
Chrysalidocarpus lutescens.
   See *Dypsis lutescens*
Clusia rosea, 38
Coccoloba uvifera, 96
Coccothrinax crinita, 79
   miraguama, 67

Cochlospermum vitifolium, 82
Cocos nucifera, 37
   plumosa. See *Syagrus romanzoffiana*
Cocos romanzoffianum. See
   Syagrus romanzoffiana
Colpothrinax wrightii, 72
Comocladia dentata, 50
Copernicia baileyana, 100
   macroglossa, 57
   torreana, 57
Cordia gerascanthus, 97
   sebestena, 98
Crescentia cujete, 54
Cycas circinalis, 75

Delonix regia, 44
Dendrocereus nudiflorus, 4
Dypsis lutescens, 71

Erythrina spp., 86

Ficus aurea, 56
   benjamina, 61
   lirata, 43
   pandurata, 43
   religiosa, 6

Gastrococos crispa, 39
Gaussia princeps, 78
Genipa americana, 55
Gliricidia sepium, 19
Guazuma tomentosa, 51
   ulmifolia, 51

Hebestigma cubense, 46
Hibiscus elatus. See *Talipariti elatum*
Hildegardia cubensis, 48
Hura crepitans, 93

Kigelia africana, 13
   pinnata, 13

Lagerstromia speciosa, 87
Livistona chinensis, 74

Magnolia grandiflora, 63
Mangifera indica, 66
Mastichodendron foetidissimum.
   See *Sideroxylon foetidissimum*
Melia azedarach, 83
Microcycas calocoma, 76
Mimosa lebbek. See *Albizia lebbek*

Nectandra coriacea, 35

Ochroma lagopus, 81
   pyramidale, 81
Oreodoxa regia. See
   Roystonea regia

Peltophorum ferrugineum, 45
   pterocarpum, 45
Persea americana, 3
   gratisima, 3
Petitia domingensis, 90
Phoenix roebelenii, 42
Phyllocarpus septentrionalis, 27
Picramnia pentandra, 5
Pimenta dioica, 84
Pinus caribaea var. *caribaea*, 85
Plumeria rubra, 62
Pouteria sapota, 65
Pseudobombax ellipticum, 28
Pseudophoenix sargentii, 77
Psidium guajava, 53

Quercus cubana, 41
   oleoides subsp. *sagraeana*, 41
   virginiana, 41

Ravenala madagascariensis, 16
Roystonea regia, 80

Sabal palmetto, 73
Samanea saman, 7

Schefflera actinophylla. See *Brassaia actinophylla*
Sideroxylon foetidissimum, 58
Simaruba glauca, 47
Spathodea campanulata, 95
Sterculia apetala, 11
  cubensis. See *Hildegardia cubensis*
Swietenia mahagoni, 25

Syagrus romanzoffiana, 36

Tabebuia angustata, 89
  chrysantha, 88
  heterophylla, 91
  pentaphylla, 91
Talipariti elatum, 64
Terminalia catappa, 10
Theobroma cacao, 21

Thrinax parviflora, 49
  radiata, 49
Trichilia hirta, 59
Trichospermum mexicanum, 52
Triplaris americana, 94

Veitchia merrillii, 2
Vitex parviflora, 92